W9-BXY-832

THE
Northampton Wools
KNITTING BOOK

THE
Northampton
Wools

KNITTING BOOK

THE SHOP PATTERNS

Linda A. Daniels

THE COUNTRYMAN PRESS
Woodstock, Vermont

To Russ, Adrienne and Jeff
You are the lights in my life

Text copyright © 2006 by Linda A. Daniels
Interior photographs copyright © 2006 by Steve Legge
  unless otherwise indicated

First Edition

Library of Congress Cataloging-in-Publication Data has been applied for.

ISBN-13: 978-0-88150-683-9
ISBN-10: 0-88150-683-4

Book design and composition by Eugenie S. Delaney
Pattern schematics by Erin Giroux
Diagrams on pages 21 and 110 by Barbara Smullen
Interior photos by Steve Legge unless otherwise indicated
Photos of Smith College and Northampton's Main Street on page
  xi by Dylan Gaffney
Front cover photograph of Swirly Whirly Scarf (p. 21) by
KeriAnne Shaw; other pattern photographs on cover by
Steve Legge

Published by The Countryman Press, P.O. Box 748, Woodstock, VT 05091

Distributed by W. W. Norton & Company, Inc., 500 Fifth Avenue, New York, NY 10110

Printed in Spain by Artes Graficas Toledo

10 9 8 7 6 5 4 3 2 1

contents

foreword

Nestled in the heart of the Pioneer Valley lies a town that has become known as Paradise. It was first called that by the great singer Jenny Lind. She found Northampton so charming that she returned to it in 1852 for her honeymoon. After dinner one evening Jenny is reputed to have said to her hostess, "I know that you all sit around the table in the evening and have work or games, so I brought my knitting, for this makes me think of my home, and of my precious mama, who died recently."

Sojourner Truth, an abolitionist, operated part of the underground railroad in this area. She taught knitting and was photographed with her knitting in her lap. She sold photographs of herself to raise money to help in the battle for freedom.

Grace Coolidge, wife of President Calvin Coolidge, carried needlework with her all the time. When she was once trapped in an elevator she "happily knitted in the dark until it was discovered that she was missing."

These women exemplify the knitting heritage of Northampton. With such a rich history of knitting it is no wonder that Northampton Wools has become a favorite resource for knitters of every level. The shop has become an integral part of the town where it is not uncommon for old friends to meet and new friendships to be formed all around a table full of knitting projects. Secrets are shared, stories are told, and problems are solved while the quiet clicking of knitting needles goes on. Knitting has become a way of connecting with each other and with our past. It also promises a connection with our future as the garments we make are worn and cherished by those we love.

This book is the result of the connection between Northampton Wools and the people who knit here. I hope you find the patterns in this book worthy of your creative energy, and that you use them as a way to express your love of the craft.

No matter where you take your knitting (or where it may take you), whatever your reason for knitting, keep in mind these words from Grace Coolidge: "Many a time when I have needed to hold myself firmly, I have taken my needle, it might be a sewing needle, some knitting needles, or a crochet hook; whatever its form or purpose it often proved to be as the needle of the compass, keeping me to the course."

—Linda A. Daniels

acknowledgments

THIS BOOK CAME INTO BEING AT THE suggestion (or should I say prompting) of Linda Roghaar, who became my agent and friend. I thank her for her insistence and assistance in getting this book together.

Thank you to Kermit Hummel and Jennifer Thompson at The Countryman Press who made this book a reality.

Without the support of KeriAnne Shaw, this book would still be just an idea. Her encouragement and enthusiasm helped me through to the end. Her contributions to the book go beyond the several patterns she created and I thank her from the bottom of my heart.

Robin Gunn was an essential part of the writing of this book. Her willingness to do anything I asked of her made light work of the many tasks associated with the book's production. She made even the hard parts seem easy. My thanks to her go beyond words.

Diane (Decker) Smith, my soul sister, was always there when I needed another pair of hands to knit the next sample.

Many thanks to Becca Steiner for her computer help and her devotion to Northampton Wools, Too.

The photography of Steven Legge made the sweaters come alive. I thank him for his expertise and sense of humor. My thanks to Dylan Gaffney and Chuck Braun who both helped at the last minute.

My deepest thanks to Marianne Snow, Brooksley Williams, and Susan Shabo who helped with the knitting that had to be done for this book.

I am very grateful to the many people who agreed to be models, sometimes on the spur of the moment: Valerie and Justin Vedovelli, Jill Thorsen, Donna Kenny, Allison Kapinto, Melinda and Alexander Calianos, Bonnie Otto, Amelia and Will St. John, Fil Inocencio Jr., John and Aidan Urschel, Trina Rondina, William Letendre, Tanya Rapinchuk, Chrissy Noh, Adrienne Daniels, Richard Hardie, Jason Grimes, and Julia Mines.

My continued thanks to the Eric Carle Museum and the Eileen Fisher store.

Lastly to all my customers and friends who have made the life I have chosen such a sweet one.

introduction

W HO WOULD HAVE BELIEVED THAT I would be sitting in front of the television watching Michael Caine accept the Oscar for best supporting actor while a giant picture of him wearing a vest that I designed and knit was flashed behind him? This was certainly the highlight of my knitting career.

I had begun to work at Northampton Wools in 1982, just a year after it had opened. Within a few months it was clear to me that I had found my calling. I loved everything about knitting and it seemed to be in my blood. In 1987, when the original owner was ready to sell, I was not in a position to buy, and so I found myself working for a yarn store owner who did not know how to knit. Her psychic had told her that owning a yarn shop would be good for her. In ten months my situation had changed and I was able to buy Northampton Wools. I felt complete.

When the film crew for *The Cider House Rules* came to town they contacted me about knitting for the costume department. I met with Renée Kalfus, the costume designer, and we chose yarns and styles. I was sent measurements for the sweaters but I never got to meet any of the stars. Charlize Theron wears two of my designs in the movie. When my husband and I went to see the film on its opening night in Northampton, I could hardly pay attention to the actual movie. I could only see the sweaters as they moved across the screen.

I have been designing sweaters almost since the beginning of my knitting experience. Often a customer will bring in a favorite but worn-out garment and ask me to write a pattern for it. Sometimes I design a sweater based on a particular yarn and what I think should be done with it. Most often the inspiration for a design comes from the customers at Northampton Wools. A request for a particular neckline or a certain fit to a sleeve can result in a pattern created just for them.

Luscious yarn ready to be knit at Northampton Wools

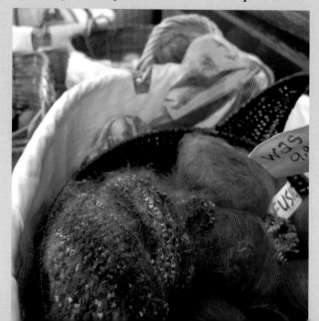

The main gates of Smith College in Northampton

This book is a collection of patterns that have become favorites of knitters over the twenty-odd years of the shop's existence. The patterns in "The Little Things" chapter have been used by students at Smith College and as teaching tools in the classes offered at the shop. The patterns from "The Simple Sweaters" chapter have been knit by beginners and experienced knitters alike when the need for some relaxing but satisfying knitting has arisen. Tackle the patterns in the "Stitch Pattern Sweaters" chapter when you're ready for a little more of a challenge. They will provide any knitter with interesting but not too difficult knitting.

Lastly, "The Birth of a Baby Store" chapter will inspire every knitting mother and her relatives to knit. I have included some of the most popular designs in this part of the book. Many of my customers love to knit for children because the knitting goes quickly. Several customers have even started baby hope chests where they store the things they have made. Whenever there is a baby shower they are prepared with a hand-knit item already made.

Whatever your reason for knitting I hope this book will inspire you. My experience has been that one never knows where a little thing like knitting can lead.

Northampton's Main Street

1. the Little Things

KeriAnne and I exchange knowing looks as the young woman at the counter says, "I want to knit a sweater for my boyfriend." The many times that we have heard about breakups happening after the completion of hours of knitting verifies the curse of the knitted sweater. This phenomenon has been written about before, and working in a yarn shop has given us first-hand knowledge of this painful truth. When the knitter is gently warned and is offered other tales of knitters and their missing sweaters the response is usually, "That won't happen to me; we have been together for a very long time." Unfortunately we later learn that the relationship has ended and the sweater has gone with the intended. I have to wonder if every time that sweater is worn the woman who made it is remembered, small consolation for the effort involved in knitting it. One student even reported that just the offer of making the new boyfriend a sweater was enough to end the dating. "The look that came over his face when I said I would knit something for him made my knitting needles freeze!" she exclaimed.

However, these stories are not enough to diminish the desire to create something by hand for the special person in one's life. So I designed several projects that will satisfy the knitter's need, but not be overly time consuming. If the breakup occurs before the project is completed, it will not matter since a scarf will fit anyone. It is a lot easier to watch a scarf or a hat walk away than it is to bid goodbye to a sweater. Take a deep breath, ask yourself if the recipient is "knitworthy," then warm up those knitting needles and cast on.

The projects in this chapter are not just for those knitters in the throes of love. Many of the knitters at Smith College have chosen the Reversible Cabled Scarf as their first foray into cabling. The Fingerless Mitts have graced the hands of many a Northampton diva over the past few years. The Montera Socks have become a staple in the wardrobes of the Birkenstock diehards, since sandals often need a little help keeping feet warm in winter. These little projects are both quick and portable and will be greeted with oohs of delight and a return of the affection with which they were knit. After all, it really is the little things that count.

blithefully yours scarf

The large number of stitches, the small needles, and the luxurious feel of camel hair combine to make this scarf a favorite of knitters needing to put a lot of love into their work. It is very easy to knit, but the result is sure to impress even those with the most discerning taste.

FINISHED MEASUREMENT: 86" long by 6" wide not including fringe.

MATERIALS: Classic Elite Yarns Blithe (100% baby camel, 128 yds), 1 sk each of colors 690, 686, 685, 681, and 675

NEEDLES: Size 6 (4mm), 29" circular needle, crochet hook for fringe

GAUGE: 20 sts and 24 rows = 4"

STRIPE PATTERN:
Rows 1–6: Knit with color 690.
Rows 7–12: Knit with color 686.
Rows 13–18: Knit with color 685.
Rows 19–24: Knit with color 681.
Rows 25–30: Knit with color 675.

This scarf is knit lengthwise in garter stitch back and forth on a circular needle.

With color A (690) and circular needle cast on 420 sts (see *Tip*). Do not join; work in garter stitch, completing the sequence of the above stripe pattern twice. Work 5 more rows with color 690. Bind off all sts evenly.

FRINGE:
Holding one strand of each color together wrap them all around a 4-inch piece of cardboard 30 times. Cut through all strands at one end. Take 6–10 strands of the yarn and fold in half. With the crochet hook, pull the fold through the edge of the scarf and then pull the ends of the strands through the fold. Pull tightly to secure. Place a fringe group in every stripe across both short edges of the scarf.

> ❖ **TIP** ❖ To cast on a large number of sts using the long tail cast on, work with two strands of yarn, either from two different balls of yarn or from both ends of the same ball.
>
> Tie the two ends of the balls together and place the knitting needle between the two strands of yarn. Hold the two yarns in the left hand just as for the long tail cast on. (See directions for the long tail cast on in your favorite knitting reference book.) Cast on the desired number of sts, then cut one ball of yarn leaving a 6-inch tail. When the knitting is finished, untie the knot from the beginning of the cast on and work both ends into the knitting.

reversible cabled scarf

The magic of cabling over ribbing solves the dilemma of a scarf with right and wrong sides. The cables are twisted on one row but give the same look on both sides so that this scarf can be worn wrapped, tied, or hanging straight.

FINISHED MEASUREMENT: 7" wide by 48" long

MATERIALS: 5 sks Karabella Aurora 8, (100% wool, 98 yds)

NEEDLES: Size 7 (4.5 mm) needles, cable needle

Cast on 60 sts.

Rows 1–9: [P2, K2] repeat to end of row.

Row 10: P2, K2 for 10 sts, slip next 4 sts (a K2 and a P2) to cable needle and hold in back, K2, P2 from needle, then K2, P2 from cable needle, work 8 sts in K2, P2 rib, slip next 4 sts to cable needle and hold in back, K2, P2 from needle, then K2, P2 from cable needle, work next 8 sts in K2, P2 rib, slip next 4 sts to cable needle and hold in back, K2, P2 from needle, then K2, P2 from cable needle, work remaining 10 sts in K2, P2 rib.

Repeat rows 1–10 until desired length, ending with row 9. Bind off in K2, P2 rib pattern.

> ❖ **TIP** ❖ When joining new ends on a scarf it is better to join in the body of the knitting rather than at the edges. This will ensure a smooth edge and the ends will hide more completely when they are worked into the ribbing.

two colors two hands hat

I designed this hat to teach knitters how to knit with two colors, one held in each hand. It has been amazing to watch people learn to knit with both hands so quickly. I think that knitting with the hand one is what knitters are accustomed to and then adding another color in the other hand fools the brain and suddenly both hands are working smoothly. The simple repeat of three and one gives both hands a workout and a rest. The result is a fabric that is doubly warm and great for the slopes or the next snowball fight.

SIZES: Child (Adult)

FINISHED MEASUREMENTS: 20½ (23)"

GAUGE: 20 sts = 4" in color pattern

NEEDLES: Size 8 (5mm) 16" circular needle, yarn needle

MATERIALS: Brown Sheep Lamb's Pride Worsted (85% wool, 15% mohair, 190 yds) in a dark and a light color

With circular needle and dark color cast on 80 (90) sts. Place marker on right-hand needle and join, being careful not to twist sts. Work in St st for 1½ inches. P one round for turning ridge. K the next round, increasing in every 10th st by knitting into the row below, to 88 (100) sts.

Begin two-color pattern stitch as follows:

Rnd 1: *K3 dark, K1 light, repeat from * around.

Rnd 2: K1 light, K1 dark, *K3 light, K1 dark, repeat from * around, end with K2 light.

Rnd 3: *K3 dark, K1 light, repeat from * around.

Rnd 4: K1 dark, *K1 light, K3 dark, repeat from * around, end with K2 dark.

Rnd 5: *K3 light, K1 dark, repeat from * around.

Rnd 6: K1 dark, * K1 light, K3 dark, repeat from * around, end with K2 dark.

Repeat these 6 rounds until the piece measures 8 (9) inches.

CLOSING THE TOP:

Turn the hat inside out. Divide the sts in half, placing 44 (50) sts on each side of the circular needle. With a third needle and using the dark color, work a three needle bind off across all sts. Secure yarn. Turn the hat to the right side. Sew the two corners of the hat together and tack them down to the middle of the hat.

Turn the hem up to the inside of the hat and sl st all around.

Block the hat by wetting it completely in cool water and placing it on a bowl or balloon of the appropriate size.

foxy hat and scarf

One of the thrills of owning a yarn shop is opening boxes of new and tempting yarns. I am often so excited by a yarn that I can't wait to work with it. When Plymouth Yarns introduced Foxy my head was already full of ideas. The yarn is made to look and feel like fur, but is completely animal-friendly since it is made of acrylic. This hat and scarf set is easy to knit and will add a touch of elegance to any winter wardrobe.

SIZE: One size fits most

MATERIALS: Plymouth Yarns Foxy (100% acrylic, 17 yds), Classic Elite Yarns Montera (50% wool, 50% llama, 127 yds)

NEEDLES: One pair size 13 (9 mm) needles, one set double pointed needles size 9 (5 mm), and one 16" circular needle size 9 (5 mm).

GAUGE: 16 sts = 4" on size 9 (5 mm) needles in St st with Montera for hat *(Gauge is not essential with the Foxy.)*

Foxy Hat

With size 13 needles and Foxy cast on 37 sts. Work back and forth in garter st until all of one sk is used up. Piece should measure about 4 inches long. Change to size 9 circular needle and with Montera knit across the row, increasing in every stitch to 74 sts. (Increase by knitting into the front and back of every stitch.) Place marker on needle and join into a round, being careful not to twist the sts. Knit the next round and increase in every 12th stitch 6 times to 80 sts.

Work in St st until piece measures 8 inches from the cast on edge.

DECREASE FOR THE TOP:
Rnd 1: *K8, K2tog, repeat from * around.
Rnd 2: Knit.
Rnd 3: *K7, K2tog, repeat from * around.
Rnd 4: Knit.
Rnd 5: *K6, K2tog, repeat from * around.
Rnd 6: Knit.

Continue to decrease on every other rnd, having 1 less st between the decreases until there are 8 sts left. Cut yarn and pull through remaining sts and tighten. Work in ends. Sew the edges of the Foxy brim together.

Foxy Scarf

With size 13 needles and Foxy cast on 3 sts.

Knit 1 row. Mark the beginning of the next row with a colored yarn to identify the increase side. Increase 1 st at the beginning of this row. Knit the next row. Repeat these two rows until there are 12 sts on the needle. Place a safety pin at the beginning of the next row. Knit until all of 1 ball of Foxy is used up. Place a second safety pin at this point. Measure the distance between pins and record this measurement. Join a second ball of Foxy and knit to the same length as the recorded measurement (start measuring from the second pin). Decrease 1 st at the beginning of the row that is on the same side that the increases were made. Decrease on every other row until there are 3 sts left. Bind off. Work in ends and wear with attitude!

fingerless mitts

These mitts add a touch of class to any outfit. They are made with hand-dyed 100% bamboo yarn and are so soft you'll forget you have them on. The increases and decreases are very specific so that the ribbing pattern is maintained throughout. This project is for the more experienced knitter, but you'll want to make more than one set.

SIZE: One size fits all

MATERIALS: 1 sk Alchemy Yarns Hand-Dyed Bamboo (100% bamboo, 140 yds)

NEEDLES: 1 set double pointed needles size 4 (3 mm), stitch marker, scrap yarn, yarn needle

GAUGE: 24 sts = 4" in ribbing pattern

Long Cuff Version

With double pointed needles cast on 12 sts on first needle, 12 sts on second needle, and 16 sts on third needle. Join, being careful not to twist sts and work 4 rounds of K1, P1 ribbing.

Decrease Rnd 1: P2tog, K1, P1 to the last 2 sts, SSK.

Work 4 rounds in ribbing pattern.

Decrease Rnd 2: K2tog, P1, K1 to the last 2 sts, P2tog.

Work 4 rounds in ribbing pattern.

Decrease Rnd 3: P2tog, K1, P1 to the last 2 sts, SSK.

Work 4 rounds in ribbing pattern.

Decrease Rnd 4: K2tog, P1, K1 to the last 2 sts, P2tog.

Work 4 rounds in ribbing pattern.

Decrease Rnd 5: P2tog, K1, P1 to the last 2 sts, SSK.

There should be 30 sts remaining and piece should measure about 3½ inches.

Work 6 rnds even in ribbing pattern.

Increase Rnd 1: K into the P bump on the first st, P the st, K1, P1 to the last st, K into the front and back of the last st.

K1, P1 for 2 rnds.

Increase Rnd 2: P into the row below the first st, then K that stitch, P1, K1 to the last st, Make 1, K the last st.

Work in P1, K1 ribbing for 2 rnds.*

Repeat from * to * 3 times. (A total of 18 more rnds.) Then work 4 more rnds even.

THUMB SHAPING:

Work 5 sts and thread them onto a piece of scrap yarn, work in ribbing pattern to the last 5 sts, and place these sts on scrap yarn as well. Put 4 twisted loops onto the right-hand needle to replace the sts on the holder. Join into a rnd and continue in ribbing pattern for 20 rnds. Bind off all sts.

THUMB:

With RS facing place the last 5 sts that were put on the scrap yarn onto a needle, attach yarn, and work them in ribbing as they appear. Place the second 5 sts onto another needle and work across those sts in pattern. With a third needle pick up and knit 4 sts across the 4 cast on sts from the thumb opening. Work in K1, P1 ribbing around all sts for 8 rnds. Bind off all sts. Work in ends. Make second mitt the same.

Short Cuff Version

Cast on 40 sts as for the long version and work 10 rnds of K1, P1 ribbing. Work increase rnds as for the longer version, then work the rest of the mitt the same as for the longer version.

fancy watch cap

KeriAnne Shaw has worked at Northampton Wools for a number of years. She began her knitting journey by taking classes and soon began to design on her own. She is an expert in the details of knitting and this watch cap is a great example of her love of getting it just right. This project may be small, but it is full of techniques for the more experienced knitter.

Like any small city, Northampton has had its share of graffiti artists. To help put an end to this some of the buildings in the downtown area have murals painted on them. The wall in the alleyway next to the store was painted by high school students with a musical theme. We photographed this hat on Fil Inocencio, Jr., in front of this mural. He is a new knitter, taught to knit by his friend Brooksley. The first thing he made was a set of wrist cuffs, which he wears with pride.

FINISHED SIZE: Because of the stretchiness of ribbing, the watch cap will fit heads that measure from 19–25".

MATERIALS: 2–3 sks Karabella Aurora 8 (100% wool, 98 yds); 2 yards of a fine cotton waste yarn in a contrasting color

NEEDLES: Two 16" circular needles size 3 (2.75 mm) and 5 (3.5 mm); set of four double pointed needles size 5 (3.5 mm); yarn needle

GAUGE: With a rib pattern, gauge is quite difficult to determine. Leaving your fabric completely relaxed (and not forgetting to count the P sts you can't see) you should have approximately 8.5 sts = 1".

SPECIAL ABBREVIATIONS:

M1P: With tip of left-hand needle, pick up ladder between the sts from front to back, and P as normal. One stitch increased.

DDC: Slip next 2 sts knitwise at the same time, K1, pass the slipped sts over the K1. Two stitches have been decreased.

DDL: Slip 1 st knitwise, K2tog, pass the slipped st over. Two stitches have been decreased.

DDR: SSK, move the decreased st back to the left-hand needle, pass the second st on the left-hand needle over the st you just moved. Slip the resulting st back to the right-hand needle. Two stitches have been decreased.

Single Rib Pattern: K1, P1.

With waste yarn and 16-inch size 3 circular needle, loosely cast on 61 sts using the long tail method (see your favorite knitting book for instructions). Tie a square knot with the 2 ends to secure. Using Aurora 8, P across all sts.

Row 1: *K1, M1P; repeat from * to the last 2 sts, K1, P1. (120 sts.)

Place a marker and join, being careful not to twist the sts.

Rnd 1: *K1, wyif, sl the next st purlwise; rep from * to marker.

Rnd 2: *Wyib sl the next st purlwise, P1, rep from * to marker.

Rnd 3: *K1, wyif sl the next st purlwise, rep from * to marker. Turn. (*Note:* This is not a typo. Turn and knit in the opposite direction so that what was the RS will now become the WS).

Work in single rib pattern (K1, P1) for 3 rnds.

Change to size 5 circular needles. Continue in rib until piece measures 2⅓ inches from the beginning.

Change to size 3 circular needle. Continue in single rib pattern until piece measures 4½ inches from the beginning.

Change to size 5 circular needle. Continue in rib pattern until piece measures 9 inches from the beginning.

Decrease for crown: (change to double pointed needles when necessary)

Rnd 1: *K1, P1, DDR, P1, (K1, P1) 5 times, DDL, P1; rep entire sequence from * five times more. (96 sts).

Rnds 2 & 3: Work in single rib as before.

Rnd 4: *K1, P1, DDR, P1, (K1, P1) 3 times, DDL, rep the entire sequence from * five times more. (72 sts).

Rnds 5 & 6: Work single rib as before.

Rnd 7: * K1, P1, DDR, P1, K1, P1, DDL, P1; rep entire sequence from * five times more (48 sts).

Rnds 8 & 9: Work in single rib as before.

Rnd 10: *K1, DDC; rep from * to end of rnd (24 sts).

Rnds 11 & 12: Knit.

Rnd 13: DDC around (8 sts).

FINISHING:

Cut yarn, leaving a 6-inch tail. Thread onto a yarn needle and weave through remaining 8 sts, pull tight. Sew around once more to secure. Weave in securely. Carefully cut out waste yarn—do not cut Aurora 8. Weave in end at the beginning of the hat. Don't forget, the bottom edge will be turned up into a cuff so you will want to weave in that end on the outside. Weave the other ends on the inside.

montera socks

These socks are on the bulky side, but wear well with sandals and clogs, the standard Northampton footwear. They are very cozy for wearing after skiing or playing in the snow and are perfect for in front of the fire. They are sized for an average woman, but can be made to fit a man's foot just by knitting the foot part longer. This has become one of the favorites of the sock knitters in town, not to mention the sock wearers.

MATERIALS: Classic Elite Yarns Montera (50% llama, 50% wool, 127 yds)

NEEDLES: Size 8 (5 mm) double pointed needles, yarn needle

LEG:
Cast on 44 sts, divide onto 3 needles. Join, being careful not to twist stitches, and work in pattern as follows:
Rnd 1: *K2, P2, rep from * around.
Rnd 2: *RT (knit into the second st on the left-hand needle, but don't slide the sts off the needle, knit into the first and slide both sts off the needle), P2, rep from * around.
   Repeat these 2 rnds until the leg measures 8 inches, or desired length.

HEEL FLAP:
Knit across 12 sts, turn. Purl back across those 12 sts and 10 more so that there are now 22 sts on one needle. Place the other 22 sts onto the front needle. Work the heel flap pattern over the first 22 sts just purled as follows:
Row 1: *Sl 1, K1, repeat from * across.
Row 2: Sl 1, P to the end.
   Repeat these 2 rows until the flap measures 2¼ inches.

TURN HEEL:
Row 1: K13 sts, K2tog, K1, turn.
Row 2: Sl 1, P5, P2tog, P1, turn.
Row 3: Sl 1, K6, K2tog, K1, turn.
Row 4: Sl 1, P7, P2tog, P1, turn.
Row 5: Sl 1, K8, K2tog, K1, turn.
Row 6: Sl 1, P9, P2tog, P1, turn.
Row 7: Sl 1, K10, K2tog, K1, turn.
Row 8: Sl 1, P11, P2tog, P1, turn.
   There should now be 14 sts left on the needle.

GUSSET:
Knit across the 14 sts of the heel, with the same needle, pick up and K 11 sts down the left side of heel flap. With an empty needle, work in pattern stitch across the 22 sts of the instep. With another empty needle, pick up and K 11 sts up the right-hand side of the heel. And with the same needle, K7 sts from the heel. The beginning of the round is now in the center back of the heel, there are 18 sts on needle 1, 22 sts on needle 2, and 18 sts on needle 3.

Rnd 1: K across 1st needle, work in pattern across the
2nd needle, K across the 3rd needle.

Rnd 2: K to the last 3 sts of the 1st needle, K2tog, K1;
work in pattern across 2nd needle, then K1, SSK,
K to end of 3rd needle.

Repeat these 2 rnds until there are 11 sts left on 1st
and 3rd needles. Work even, keeping the continuity of
the pattern stitch on needle 2 until the sock reaches
the base of the little toe when tried on, or the piece
measures 6–8 inches from the back of the heel.

SHAPE TOE:

Rnd 1: K to the last 3 sts of 1st needle, K2tog, K1, on
2nd needle K1, SSK, K to the last 3 sts, K2tog, K1;
on 3rd needle, K1, SSK, K to end.

Rnd 2: Knit.

Repeat these 2 rnds until there are 16 sts left. Knit
the sts from the 1st needle onto the 3rd needle so that
there are 8 sts on each of 2 needles. Join sts by using a
Kitchener st. (See directions for Kitchener st in your
favorite knitting reference book.) Work in any ends
and make a second sock.

swirly whirly scarf

This fun-to-knit scarf was designed by Robin Gunn. One Monday she realized that she needed a present for a birthday on Saturday, and the Swirly scarf idea was born. It soon became one of the most popular designs in the shop. Don't be intimidated by the large number of stitches, as they are not on the needle for very long. Our fastest knitter was able to bind off all the stitches in just over half an hour, so the whole thing can really be completed in a weekend.

FINISHED SIZE: 72" long

MATERIALS: 1 sk Mountain Colors Mountain Goat (55% Mohair, 45% wool; 230 yds)

NEEDLES: 29" circular needle size 11 (8 mm), yarn needle, stitch markers

GAUGE: It is not essential to this scarf.

With circular needle cast on 600 sts. Yes, I really mean 600 sts. See the *Tip* in the Blithfully Yours Scarf pattern for help, and place a marker every 100 sts to make the counting easier.

Knit 1 row.

Row 1: K2tog across the row.

Row 2: Knit.

Repeat these 2 rows twice more. 75 sts remain.

Knit 2 rows.

Row 1: Knit into the front and back of each st across.

Row 2: Knit.

Repeat these 2 rows twice. 600 sts on needle.

Bind off all sts loosely. Sew A to B together to make rounded edges (see diagram).

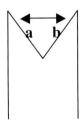

2. the Simple Sweaters

KNITTING DOESN'T HAVE TO BE COMPLICATED to be stylish, and the four sweaters in this chapter prove that. Although each of these sweaters is done in stockinette stitch, they offer the knitter an opportunity to advance their knitting skills. The man's cardigan and the Four Seasons vest have pockets done with two different techniques. The raglan shaping on the pullover adds a fully fashioned shaping to the fit, and the two-color cardigan employs a simple method of adding color. I like to think that these designs reflect the lifestyle in Northampton, a lifestyle based on simplicity but with a love of being just a little different.

FULL

Welcome
to Northampton

WHERE THE COFFEE
IS STRONG AND SO ARE
THE WOMEN©... AND THE
FIRST HOUR IN THIS
GARAGE IS ALWAYS FREE !

Have a Great Visit

cardigan with pockets

This cardigan is sure to become a favorite of the man in your life. The comfortable fit, with slightly set in sleeves and the big side pockets, the softness of the yarn, and the zippered front all combine to make this cardigan the first choice when dressing for success. Our model, Will Letendre, is known in town as the "Parking Csar." It is his task to oversee all the parking and its inherent problems in Northampton. This sign in front of the parking garage is a good indicator of the humor and sensibility that Mr. Letendre brings to his job.

SIZES: S (M, L, XL)

FINISHED MEASUREMENTS: 38 (40, 44, 48)"/96.5 (101.5, 112, 122) cm

LENGTH TO SHOULDER: 23 (24, 26, 26)"/58.5 (61,66, 66) cm

SLEEVE LENGTH: 17 (18, 18, 19)"/43 (46, 46, 48.5) cm

MATERIALS: 7 (8, 9, 9) sks Rowan Plaid (42% merino wool, 30% acrylic, 28% superfine alpaca; 109 yds)

NEEDLES: Size 10 (6 mm) and 11 (7 mm) straight needles, 4 stitch holders, separating zipper, yarn needle

GAUGE: 12 sts = 4", 15 rows = 4" in St st with size 11 needles

BACK:
With size 10 needles, cast on 57 (60, 66, 72) sts. Work in K1, P1 ribbing for 11 rows. Change to larger needles and work in St st until piece measures 13 (14, 15, 15) inches or desired length to underarm. End with a WS row.

SHAPE ARMHOLES:
With RS facing, bind off 4 sts at the beginning of the next 2 rows.
Row 1: K2, K2tog, K to last 4 sts, SSK, K2.
Row 2: Purl.
   Repeat these 2 rows 5 more times. 37 (40, 46, 52) sts remain.
   Work even in St st until armhole measures 10 (10, 11, 11) inches. Place remaining sts on a holder.

LEFT FRONT:
With smaller needles, cast on 28 (30, 33, 36) sts. Work in K1, P1 ribbing for 11 rows. Change to larger needles.
Increase for pocket: K6, K in front and back of the next 20 (22, 25, 28) sts, K2.
Next row: P2 and sl these sts to a holder, *move yarn to the back and sl the next st to the holder, move yarn to the front and P1, repeat from * across to the last 6 sts. Sl these last 6 sts to the same holder without working them.

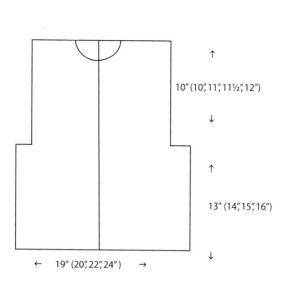

10" (10", 11", 11½", 12")

13" (14", 15", 16")

← 19" (20", 22", 24") →

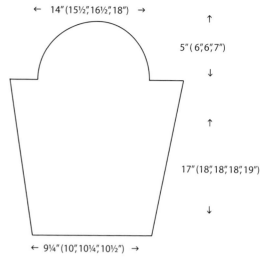

← 14" (15½", 16½", 18") →

5" (6", 6", 7")

17" (18", 18", 18", 19")

← 9¼" (10", 10¼", 10½") →

POCKET:

Working across the sts on the needle:

Row 1: Work in P1, K1 ribbing to end.

Row 2: P to the last 5 sts, K1, P1, K1, P1, K1.

Repeat these 2 rows until pocket measures 6 inches above ribbing. Cut yarn leaving a long tail and place these sts on another holder.

Return to the sts on the first holder and place them on one of the smaller needles so that you are ready to P a row. Attach yarn and with the larger needle, P across the 28 (30, 33, 36) sts of front. Continue in St st until the front measures 6 inches from the ribbing, ending with a P row.

JOINING THE POCKET TO THE FRONT:

Place the pocket sts onto a smaller needle so that the two needles are pointing in the same direction as the front needle. K6 sts from the large needle, then holding the 2 needles together knit 1 st from the front needle together with 1 st from the back needle. Work across all sts in this manner to the last 2 sts. K2.

Continue in St st until the front is the same length as the back to the underarm. End with a P row.

SHAPE ARMHOLE:

Bind off 4 sts at the beginning of the next row.

Purl 1 row.

Row 1: K2, K2tog, K to end.

Row 2: Purl.

Repeat these 2 rows 5 more times. Work even in St st until armhole measures 7 (7, 8, 8) inches. End with a K row.

SHAPE NECK:

Bind off 6 sts at beg of next row.

Next row: K to the last 4 sts, SSK, K2.

Purl 1 row.

Repeat these last 2 rows until 12 (13, 14, 16) sts remain. Place these sts on a holder.

RIGHT FRONT:

With smaller needles cast on 28 (30, 33, 36) sts. Work in K1, P1 ribbing for 11 rows. Change to larger needle.

INCREASE FOR POCKET:

K2, K into the front and back of each of the next 20 (22, 25, 28) sts, K6.

Next row: P6 and place these sts on a holder, * move yarn to back, slip next st to holder, P1, repeat from * to the last 2 sts, place these 2 sts on the holder without Purling them.

POCKET:

Row 1: (RS) K to the last 5 sts, P1, K1, P1, K1, P1.

Row 2: Work in K1, P1 ribbing to end.

Repeat these 2 rows until pocket measures 6 inches from the top of the ribbing. Cut yarn leaving a long tail, and place these sts on a holder.

Return to the sts on the first holder, and slip these sts to a smaller needle. Attach yarn and with the larger needle P across all sts. Work in St st until front measures 6 inches above the ribbing, ending with a P row.

JOIN POCKET TO FRONT:

Place the pocket sts onto a smaller needle so that the 2 needles are pointing in the same direction. K2 sts from the front needle, then K1 st from the front needle together with one st from the back needle to

the last 6 sts. K these 6 sts.

Continue in St st until piece measures the same as the back to the underarm.

End with a K row.

SHAPE ARMHOLE:

Bind off 4 sts at the beg of the next row.

Row 1: K to the last 4 sts, SSK, K2.

Row 2: Purl.

Repeat these 2 rows 5 times.

Work even in St st until armhole measures 7 (7, 8, 8) inches, ending with a P row.

SHAPE NECK:

Bind off 6 sts, K to end.

Purl 1 row.

Row 1: K2, K2tog, K to end.

Row 2: Purl.

Repeat these 2 rows until 12 (13, 14, 16) sts remain. Place these sts on a holder.

SLEEVES:

With smaller needles cast on 28 (30, 32, 34) sts. Work in K1, P1 ribbing for 11 rows. Change to larger needles and work in St st. Increase 1 st at the beg and end of the next row and then every following 4th row 7 (8, 9, 10) times. Work even until sleeve measures 17 (18, 18, 19) inches from beginning.

SHAPE ARMHOLE:

Bind off 4 sts at the beg of the next 2 rows.

Row 1: K2, K2tog, K to the last 4 sts, SSK, K2.

Row 2: Purl.

Repeat these 2 rows until sleeve cap measures 5, (6, 6, 7) inches. Bind off all sts.

FINISHING:

Join fronts to back at shoulders using the three needle bind off method as described in the *Glossary*.

NECK: With RS facing and using the smaller needles, pick up and K 12 (13, 14, 15) sts along right front, K across sts from back neck holder, pick up and K 12 (13, 14, 15) sts along left front neck edge. Work in K1, P1 ribbing for 7 rows. Bind off in ribbing.

Sew sleeves to body matching the center of the sleeve to the shoulder seam and matching the bound off sts at each underarm. Sew side and sleeve seams.

FRONT BANDS: With RS facing, pick up and K 3 sts for every 4 rows along right front edge, K and bind off the next row. Repeat for left front edge. This provides a stable edge for the zipper.

Measure the front length from start of the neck shaping to the cast on edge. This is the length of the zipper that you will need. Hand-sew the zipper in place being sure to place the knitted edge on the outside of the teeth so that the knitted fabric does not cover the teeth.

two-color cardigan

Using color in simple ways can have a dramatic effect when the colors are right. This two-color cardigan is simple to knit, and the trick of layering the pieces is very easy to do. Even the buttons are a snap—there are no buttonholes to make, just sew the buttons through both layers of fabric and pull the sweater on.

Melinda is shown here in front of the Calvin Theatre in downtown Northampton. The theatre is named for Calvin Coolidge and used to be a movie theatre. Now it is one of the premier live performance venues in the region with acts like Dar Williams, James Taylor, Nancy Griffith, and even the Monkees.

SIZES: S (M, L, XL)

FINISHED MEASUREMENTS: 38 (40, 42, 44)"/96.5 (101.5, 107, 112) cm

LENGTH TO SHOULDER: 19 (20½, 22, 22)"/48 (52, 56, 56) cm

SLEEVE LENGTH: 17 (17, 18, 18)"/43 (43, 46, 46) cm.

MATERIALS: Rowan Yarns Summer Tweed (70% silk, 30% cotton, 117 yds); 7 (8, 9, 9) sks in MC, 2 sks in CC

NEEDLES: Size 7 (4.5 mm) or size needed to obtain gauge, yarn needle, 2 stitch holders, one 29" circular needle size 6 (4 mm), 3 1-inch buttons

GAUGE: 16 sts and 24 rows = 4" in St st

BACK:
With CC and size 7 needles cast on 76 (80, 84, 88) sts and work in St st for 3 inches, ending with a P row. Place all sts onto the circular needle and set aside. With MC and size 7 needles cast on 76 (80, 84, 86) sts and work in St st for 1½ inches, ending with a P row. Place the MC piece on top of the CC piece so that the RS of the CC is against the WS of the MC. Holding the 2 pieces together, with MC, K1 stitch from the MC needle with 1st from the CC needle across the row so that the pieces are joined and there are 76 (80, 84, 88) sts left on one needle. Continue in St st with MC until piece measures 10 (11, 12, 12) inches from joining row, ending with a P row.

SHAPE ARMHOLE:
Bind off 6 sts at the beg of next 2 rows. Work even in St st until armhole measures 9 (9½, 10, 10) inches from bind off. Place all sts on a holder.

LEFT FRONT:
With CC cast on 38 (40, 42, 44) sts and work in St st for 3 inches, ending with a P row. Place all sts onto the circular needle and set aside. With MC cast on 38 (40, 42, 44) sts and work in St st until piece measures 1½ inches, ending with a P row. Join the two pieces together as for the back. Continue in St st with MC until front measures the same length as the back to the underarm, ending with a P row.

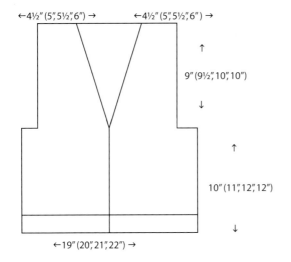

←4½" (5", 5½", 6") →   ←4½" (5", 5½", 6") →

9" (9½", 10", 10")

10" (11", 12", 12")

←19" (20", 21", 22") →

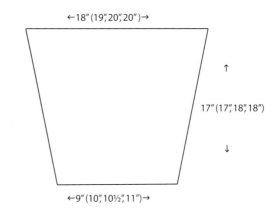

←18" (19", 20", 20")→

17" (17", 18", 18")

←9" (10", 10½", 11")→

SHAPE ARMHOLE:
Bind off 6 sts at the beg of the next row.
P one row.

SHAPE NECK:
Decrease 1 st at the neck edge as follows:
Row 1: K to the last 3 sts, SSK, K1.
Row 2: Purl.
Repeat these 2 rows until 18 (20, 22, 24) sts remain. Work even until piece measures the same as the back. Place remaining sts on a holder.

RIGHT FRONT:
Work as for left front ending with a K row at the armhole shaping. Bind off 6 sts at the beg of the next row (a P row).

SHAPE NECK:
Decrease 1 st at the neck edge as follows:
Row 1: K1, K2tog, K to end.
Row 2: Purl.

Repeat these 2 rows until 18 (20, 22, 24) sts remain. Work even until piece measures the same length as the back.

SHOULDERS: Join the fronts to the back using the three needle bind off method as described in the *Glossary.*

SLEEVES:
With CC cast on 36 (40, 42, 44) sts and work in St st for 3 inches ending with a P row. Place sts onto the circular needle and set aside. With MC cast on 36 (40, 42, 44) sts and work in St st for 1½ inches ending with a P row. Join the two pieces as for the back. Continue in MC and in St st, increasing 1 st at the beg and end of the next row and then every following 4th row 20 (20, 22, 24) times until there are 76 (80, 86, 92) sts. Work even if necessary until sleeve measures 17 (17, 18, 18) inches or desired length to underarm. Bind off all sts loosely.

FINISHING

NECKBAND: With RS facing, beginning at the joining of MC and CC on the right front and with CC and circular needle, pick up and K 3 sts for every 4 rows along the right front edge to the shoulder, K across the sts from the back neck holder, pick up and K 3 sts for every 4 rows along the left front edge, stopping at the join of MC and CC.

Work 6 rows of K1, P1 ribbing. Bind off all sts.

Place right front over left front and sew 3 buttons evenly spaced through all fabric.

Pin the sleeves to the body, matching the center of the sleeve to the shoulder seam. Pin the edge of the sleeve to the corner of the front and back where the bind off is. Sew in place. Sew the first 1½ inches of the underarm sleeve seam to the bound off sts of the front and back. Sew side and underarm seams. Work in ends.

kerianne's plaid sweater

Designed by KeriAnne Shaw, this is an oversized sweater made for those relaxing days when curling up is the most work you feel like doing. Knit in a wool and alpaca blend, it is cuddly and cozy and very easy to knit. The details are all in the shaping at the raglan sleeves, which add a fashionable touch to a classic shape.

SIZES: S (M, L)

FINISHED MEASUREMENTS: 45 (47, 49)"/114 (119.5, 125) cm

LENGTH TO UNDERARM: 15 (15, 16)"/38 (38, 40.5) cm.

SLEEVE LENGTH: 17 (18, 18)"/43 (46, 46) cm

GAUGE: 12 sts and 15 rows = 4"

MATERIALS: 10 (10, 11) sks Rowan Plaid (42% merino wool, 30% acrylic, 28% superfine alpaca; 109 yds)

NEEDLES: Size 10 (6 mm) and 10½ (6.5 mm) needles, stitch holders, yarn needle

SPECIAL DECREASE NOTE:

SSP2togtbl: Sl 1 st knitwise, sl 1 st knitwise, return both sts to the left-hand needle without twisting and P these 2 sts together through the back.

BACK:

With size 10 needles, cast on 68 (71, 74) sts.
Row 1: (WS) P2, K1 across row to the last 2 sts, P2.

Row 2: (RS) K2, P1 across row to the last 2 sts, K2.
   Repeat these 2 rows 6 more times, then repeat row 1. Ribbing should measure about 3¼ inches.
   Change to larger needles and beginning with a K row work in St st for 36 rows, or until piece measures 15 (15, 16) inches from the cast on edge.

SHAPE ARMHOLES:
Bind off 3 sts at the beginning of the next 2 rows.

DECREASE ROWS:
(RS): K2, P1tbl, K2tog, K to the last 3 sts, P1 tbl, K2.
(WS): P2, K1tbl, SSP2togtbl (see *Special Decrease Note*), P to the last 3 sts, K1tbl, P2.
   Repeat these 2 decrease rows until 30 (33, 36) sts remain.

SHAPE NECK:
Next row: (RS) K2, P1tbl, K2tog, K3. Leave remaining sts on needle, turn work.
Row 2: P1, P2tog, P1, K1tbl, P2.
Row 3: K2, P1tbl, K2tog, K1.
Row 4: P2tog, K1tbl, P2.
Row 5: K2, K2tog.
Row 6: P2tog, P1.
Row 7: Bind off knitwise, cut yarn and pull through last st and tighten.
   Rejoin yarn to remaining sts and K across next 14 (17, 20) sts and place them on a holder.
Row 1: K1, K2tog, K2, P1tbl, K2.
Row 2: P2, K1tbl, SSP2togtbl, P2.

Row 3: K1, SSK, P1tbl, K2.
Row 4: P2, K1tbl, SSP2togtbl.
Row 5: K1, K2tog, K1.
Row 6: P1, P2tog.
Row 7: Bind off knitwise. Cut yarn and pull through last st to fasten off.

FRONT:

Work as for back, shaping the armholes at the same length, until 38 (41, 44) sts remain.

SHAPE NECK:

Row 1: K2, P1tbl, K2tog, K9 (11, 11), turn, leaving remaining sts on needle.
Row 2: P1, SSP2togtbl, P7 (9, 9), K1tbl, P2.
Row 3: K2, P1tbl, K2tog, K7 (9, 9), turn.
Row 4: P1, SSP2togtbl, P5 (7, 7), K1tbl, P2.
Row 5: K2, P1tbl, K2tog, K5 (7, 7), turn.
Row 6: P1, SSP2togtbl, P3 (5, 5), K1tbl, P2.
Row 7: K2, P1tbl, K2tog, K3 (5, 5), turn.
Row 8: P1, SSP2togtbl, P1 (3, 3), K1tbl, P2.
Row 9: K2, P1tbl, K2tog, K1 (3, 3), turn.

FOR SMALL:

5 sts remain.
Next row: P2tog, P3.
Next row: K2, K2tog. Bind off remaining sts.

FOR MEDIUM AND LARGE:

Row 10: P1, SSP2togtbl, P1(1), K1tbl, P2.
Row 11: K2, P1tbl, K2tog, K1(1), turn.
Row 12: P2tog, K1tbl, P2.
Row 13: K2, K2tog, turn.
Row 14: SSP2togtbl, P1.

Bind off knitwise, cut yarn and pull through last st.
Reattach yarn to remaining sts, knit across 10 (9, 12) sts and place these sts on a holder. Continue across remaining 14 (16, 16) sts as follows:
Row 1: K1, K2tog, K8 (10, 10), P1tbl, K2.
Row 2: P2, K1tbl, SSP2togtbl, P8 (10, 10).
Row 3: K1, K2tog, K6 (8, 8), P1tbl, K2.
Row 4: P2, K1tbl, SSP2togtbl, P6 (8, 8).
Row 5: K1, K2tog, K4 (6, 6), P1tbl, K2.
Row 6: P2, K1tbl, SSP2togtbl, P4 (6, 6).
Row 7: K1, K2togtbl, K2 (4, 4), P1tbl, K2.
Row 8: P2, K1tbl, SSP2togtbl, P2 (4, 4).
Row 9: K1, K2tog, K0 (2, 2), P1tbl, K2.

FOR SMALL:

5 sts remain.
Next Row: P2tog, P2.
Next Row: K2, K2tog. Bind off.

FOR MEDIUM AND LARGE:

Row 10: P2, K1tbl, SSP2togtbl, P2 (2).
Row 11: K1, SSK, P1tbl, K2 (2).
Row 12: K1, K2tog, K2.
Row 13: P2, P2tog.
Row 14: K2tog, K1.

Bind off knitwise, cut yarn and pull through the last st.

SLEEVES:

With size 10 needles cast on 35 (37, 39) sts.
Row 1: (WS) P2, K1 across row, ending with P2.
Row 2: (RS) K2, P1 across row ending with K2.

Repeat these 2 rows 4 more times, then repeat row 1.

Change to larger needles and work in St st. Increase on the 7th row and then on every following 6th row as follows:

Increase Row: K2, M1, K to the last 2 sts, M1, K2.

When there are 53 (55, 57) sts, work even until sleeve measures 17 (18, 18) inches or desired length to underarm. End with a P row.

SHAPE ARMHOLE:

Bind off 3 sts at the beg of the next 2 rows.

Work the following 2 decrease rows until 9 (11, 13) sts remain.

Row 1: K2, P1tbl, K2tog, K to the last 3 sts, P1tbl, K2.

Row 2: P2, K1tbl, SSP2togtbl, P to the last 3 sts, K1tbl, P2.

Place remaining sts on a holder.

FINISHING:

Sew sleeves to front and back. Sew side and underarm seams.

NECK:

With a 16-inch circular size 10 needle, knit across the sts from the back neck holder, pick up and K approx 9 (10, 10) sts down left front neck, knit across sts from front neck holder and pick up and K 9 (10, 10) sts up right front neck edge. Place a marker on the needle and work 4 rows of K2, P1 ribbing. Bind off in pattern. Work in ends.

four seasons vest

This easy-to-knit vest is truly wearable all year long over a T-shirt, turtleneck, or by itself. The V-neck shaping is accented by a collar and the small pocket on the front is inserted as you knit.

Tanya Rapinchuk, one of Northampton's finest midwives, models it in front of the Hestia Mural in downtown Northampton. This mural depicts the history of the women who have helped to shape Northampton such as Sojourner Truth, political activist Frances Crowe, Smith College President Ruth Simmons, and many others.

SIZE: XS (S, M, L, XL, XXL)

FINISHED MEASUREMENTS: 38 (40, 42, 44, 46, 48)"/96.5 (101.5, 106.5, 112, 117, 122) cm

LENGTH TO UNDERARM: 12 (13, 14, 14, 15, 15)"/30.5 (33, 35.5, 35.5, 38, 38) cm

MATERIALS: 6 (6, 7, 7, 8, 8) sks Classic Elite Yarns Four Seasons, (70% cotton, 30% wool; 103 yds); four buttons

NEEDLES: Size 6 (4 mm) and 8 (5 mm) straight needles, 5 stitch holders, yarn needle

GAUGE: 18 sts and 20 rows = 4" in St st on size 8 needles

BACK:
With smaller needles cast on 86 (90, 94, 98, 102, 108) sts. Work in garter st for 6 rows. Change to

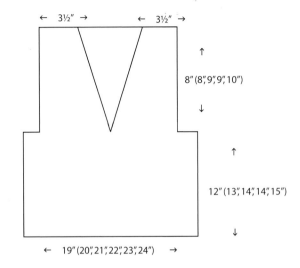

larger needles and work in St st until piece measures 12 (13, 14, 14, 15, 15) inches, or desired length to underarm. End with a WS row.

SHAPE ARMHOLE:
Bind off 10 sts at the beg of the next 2 rows.

DECREASE ROW:
K1, SSK, K to the last 3 sts, K2tog, K1.
Purl 1 row.
Repeat these 2 rows 5 (5, 7, 7, 9, 9) times more.
54 (58, 58, 62, 62, 68) sts remain. Work even until armhole measures 8 (8, 9, 9, 10, 10) inches. Place remaining sts on a holder.

LEFT FRONT:

With smaller needles, cast on 43 (45, 47, 49, 51, 53) sts. Work in garter st for 6 rows. Change to larger needles and work in St st until piece measures same as the back to the underarm. End with a WS row.

SHAPE ARMHOLE:

Bind off 10 sts at the beg of the next row. Purl 1 row.

DECREASE FOR ARMHOLE AND NECK:

K1, SSK, knit to the last 3 sts, K2tog, K1.

P 1 row.

Repeat these last 2 rows 5 (5, 7, 7, 9, 9) times more.

Continue to decrease at the neck edge:

K to the last 3 sts, K2tog, K1.

Purl 1 row.

Repeat these last 2 rows until 13 sts remain for every size. Work even until piece measures same as the back. Place all sts on a holder.

POCKET LINING:

With size 8 needles, cast on 24 sts, work in St st for 5 inches. Slip all sts to a holder.

RIGHT FRONT:

With smaller needles, cast on 43 (45, 47, 49, 51, 53) sts. Work in garter st for 6 rows. Change to larger needles and work in St st until piece measures 7 inches, ending with a WS row.

PLACE POCKET FOR ALL SIZES:

Next row: K10 sts, sl the next 24 sts to a holder, knit across the 24 sts of the pocket lining, K to the end of the row. Continue in St st until piece measures the same as the back to the underarm. End with a RS row.

SHAPE ARMHOLE:

Bind off 10 sts at the beg of the next row.

Decrease for armhole and neck edge:

K1, SSK, K to the last 3 sts, K2tog, K1.

Purl 1 row.

Repeat these last 2 rows 5 (5, 7, 7, 9, 9) times more.

Continue to decrease at neck edge:

K1, SSK, K to end.

Purl 1 row.

Repeat these last 2 rows until 13 sts remain for every size. Work even on these sts until piece measures the same length as the back. Place all sts on a holder.

Join shoulder sts using the three needle bind off method as described in the *Glossary.*

ARMHOLE EDGING:

With RS facing and smaller needles, pick up and K 3 sts for every 4 rows along the armhole, including the bound off sts. K 4 rows and bind off all sts.

Sew side seams. Sew pocket lining to inside of body. Place sts from front pocket holder onto smaller needle. Attach yarn and K 4 rows. Bind off loosely. Tack down sides of garter st border to the front body.

BUTTON BAND:

With RS facing and smaller needles, pick up and K 3 sts for every 4 rows starting at the first neck decrease to the bottom edge of the left front. Work 6 rows of garter st and bind off.

BUTTONHOLE BAND:

With RS facing and smaller needles, pick up and K 3 sts for every 4 rows starting at the bottom edge to the first neck decrease. Work garter st for 3 rows. Place 4 buttonholes evenly spaced: bind off 2 sts at each buttonhole space. On the next row, cast on 2 sts at each bound off space. K 2 more rows and bind off.

COLLAR:

With RS facing and smaller needles pick up and K 3 sts for every 4 rows starting at the first neck decrease on right front, K across sts from back neck holder, and down the left front to the first neck decrease.

Row 1: Knit.

Row 2: K4, P to last 4 sts, K4.

Repeat these 2 rows until collar measures 2¾ inches.

Change to garter st for 4 rows. Bind off all sts loosely. Work in ends. Fold collar and press lightly to set the fold. *Note:* Collar ends do not attach to front bands. Sew on buttons.

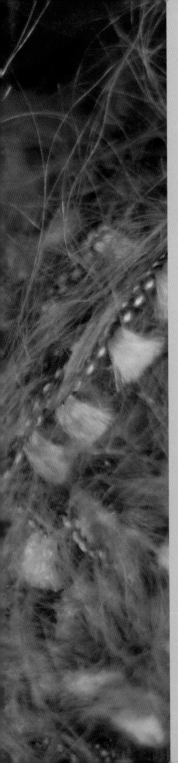

3. the Famous Favorites

S OME SWEATERS BECOME FAVORITES BECAUSE they are fun to knit, some because the fit is just right, and some because of what the design has meant while it was being created. The Guernsey sweater in this chapter has a long tradition in the knitting world; I have updated the fit and the yarn. The ribbed vest and the boat neck were both designed for *The Cider House Rules* and the Shawl Collar Cardigan was designed for a New York boutique. I hope that when you knit these they will become your favorites too.

cider house boat neck pullover

*Working for the movie **The Cider House Rules** was exciting to say the least. After completing a vest for Michael Caine and a sweater for Charlize Theron, I was delighted when the costumers asked for a second sweater that Charlize Theron would wear. Charlize wears it under a jacket at the end of the movie as she meets Tobey Maguire to say goodbye. It has become popular with the new young knitters because of its slim fit and of course the ease of knitting. The ribbing in the yoke makes it a self-finishing piece that translates into a very flattering neckline. Worked in a soft merino wool it is comfortable to wear even against the skin.*

SIZE: XS (S, M, L)

FINISHED MEASUREMENTS: 34 (36, 38, 40)"/86.5 (91.5, 96.5, 102) cm

MATERIALS: 8 (9, 10, 11) sks Jaeger Extra Fine Merino DK, by Jaeger Yarns (100% merino wool, 137 yds/50gms)

NEEDLES: Size 4 (3.5 mm) and 5 (3.75 mm) straight needles, 1 stitch holder, yarn needle

GAUGE: 22 sts and 30 rows = 4" in St st with size 5 (3.75 mm) needles

BACK AND FRONT:
With smaller needles cast on 94 (100, 104, 110) sts. Work in K2, P2 ribbing until piece measures 4 inches.

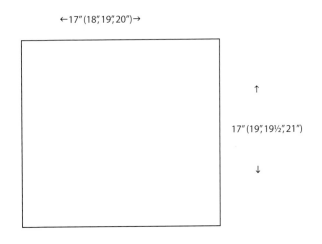

←17" (18", 19", 20")→

17" (19", 19½", 21")

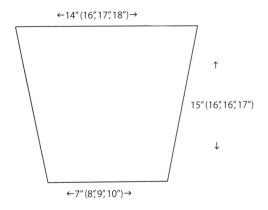

←14" (16", 17", 18")→

15" (16", 16", 17")

←7" (8", 9", 10")→

Change to larger needles and continue in St st until piece measures 10 (11, 11, 12) inches.

BEGIN YOKE AND ARMHOLE:

Work in K2, P2 ribbing until armhole measures 7 (8, 8½, 9) inches.

Next Row: Rib 24 (26, 28, 30) sts, loosely bind off the next 46 (48, 48, 50) sts. Rib the remaining 24 (26, 28, 30) sts and place all sts on a holder.

When both pieces are complete join the shoulder sts using the three needle bind off method as described in the *Glossary.*

SLEEVES:

With right side facing and using larger needles, pick up and knit 78 (88, 94, 100) sts across the yoke and armhole ribbing. Work in K2, P2 ribbing for 2 inches. Decrease 1 st at each end of the next and every following 4th row 20 (22, 24, 26) times. 38 (44, 46, 48) sts remain. Work even in ribbing as established until sleeve measures 15 (16, 16, 17) inches or desired length. Bind off all sts loosely.

Sew side and underarm seams. Work in ends.

all in rib v-neck vest

*Just as some shots end up on the cutting room floor, some costumes never make it into the movies. This vest is a good example of work done, but not used. The costumers for **The Cider House Rules** asked me to make a close-fitting vest for one of the characters, but when it was completed and tried on, they decided not to use it. The original became part of the wardrobe for Miramax and could show up in some other film down the road. In the meantime I wrote up the pattern, made another model, and knitters have been making it ever since. It is a form-fitting vest in a simple but tightly-knit stitch that requires a little bit of experience with the shaping at the armholes and for the V-neck. The word "classic" comes to mind, and comfort is what you will feel while wearing it.*

SIZES: S (M, L, XL)

FINISHED MEASUREMENTS: 34 (36, 38, 40)"/ 86.5 (91.5, 96.5, 102) cm

MATERIALS: 4 (5, 5, 6) sks Manos Del Uruguay wool by Design Source (100% wool; 138 yds/100 gms)

NEEDLES: Size 6 (4 mm) and 8 (5 mm) straight needles, one 16" circular needle size 6 (4 mm), 1 stitch holder, yarn needle

GAUGE: 20 sts and 24 rows = 4" in K2, P2 ribbing on larger needles

BACK:

With smaller needles, cast on 82 (86, 90, 94) sts. Work in K2, P2 ribbing for 1½ inches. Change to larger needles and continue in rib as established until piece measures 11 (12, 13, 14) inches or desired length to underarm.

SHAPE ARMHOLE:

Bind off 6 sts at the beg of the next 2 rows. Decrease 1 st at each end of every other row 9 (11, 13, 15) times. Work even in rib as established until armhole measures 9 (9½, 10, 11) inches. Place all sts on a holder.

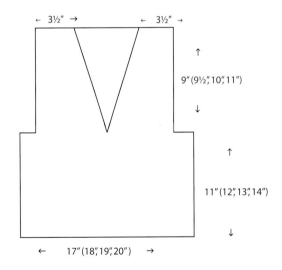

FRONT:

Work same as the back to the armhole.

SHAPE ARMHOLE AND NECK EDGE:

Bind off 6 sts at the beg of the next row, work 33 (35, 37, 39) more sts. There are now 34 (36, 38, 40) sts on the right-hand needle. Slip the next 2 sts onto a safety pin. Attach a second ball of yarn and work across the remaining sts. Bind off 6 sts at the beg of the next row. Work across the sts of the second piece in pattern as established.

Working both sides at the same time, decrease 1 st at the armhole edges every other row 9 (11, 13, 15) times. *At the same time* decrease 1 st at each neck edge every 4th row 9 times for every size. 16 sts remain for all sizes.

Work even in rib as established until front measures the same as the back.

Join the shoulder sts using the three needle bind off method as described in the *Glossary*.

Sew the side seams.

ARMHOLE FINISHING:

With circular needle and RS facing, beginning at the side seam, pick up and K2 sts for every 3 rows around the entire armhole. Count the sts and add or subtract sts to make a multiple of 4. Work in K2, P2 ribbing in the round for 1 inch. Bind off all sts loosely.

V-NECK FINISHING:

With RS facing and circular needle, K across the sts from the back neck holder, pick up and K3 sts for every 4 rows down the left front neck edge, K2 sts tog from the safety pin, place marker, pick up and K 3 sts for every 4 rows up the right front neck edge.

Place a different colored marker for the beg of the round. Work in K2, P2 ribbing until 2 sts before the marker. Slip the next 2 sts knitwise, remove marker, K1, pass the slipped sts over the K1, replace marker on right-hand needle and continue in K2, P2 ribbing to end of round. Repeat this V-neck decrease round until ribbing measures 1 inch. Bind off in ribbing pattern. Work in ends.

shawl collar cardigan

This cardigan is for the more experienced knitter. The cable twists and turns, with a wrapped center that it looks as if it is tied. The collar requires some knowledge of short row shaping and how to deal with the wraps. The yarn is kettle-dyed, so there are variations in the color that add to the beauty and depth of the cables.

SIZES: S (M, L, XL, XXL)

FINISHED MEASUREMENTS: 36 (40, 44, 48, 52)"/91.5 (102, 112, 122, 132) cm

MATERIALS: 8 (9, 10, 11, 12) sks Manos Del Uruguay by Design Source, 100% wool (145 yds/100 gms) 6 ¾-inch buttons

NEEDLES: One pair size 8 (5 mm) and size 10 (6 mm) needles, one 29" circular needle size 8 (5 mm), yarn needle, markers, stitch holders, cable needle

GAUGE: 16 sts and 28 rows = 4" in St st

TWISTED AND CROSSED CABLE PATTERN (worked over 16 sts)

Row 1: (RS) P2, C4B, (sl 2 sts to cn, hold in back, K2, K 2 sts from cn), P4, C4F, (sl 2 sts to cn, hold in front, K2, K2 from the cn), P2.

Row 2: K2, P4, K4, P4, K2.

Row 3: P1, T3B (sl 1 st to cn, hold in back, K2, P1 from the cn), T3F (sl 2 sts to the cn, hold in front, P1, K2 from cn), P2, T3B, T3F, P1.

Row 4: K1, [P2, K2] 3 times, P2, K1.

Row 5: [T3B, P2, T3F] twice.

Row 6: P2, K4, P4, K4, P2.

Row 7: K2, P4, C4B, P4, K2.

Row 8: As the 6th row.

Row 9: K2, P4, K4, P4, K2.

Row 10: As the 6th row.

Row 11: As the 7th row.

Row 12: As the 6th row.

Row 13: [T3F, P2, T3B] twice.

Row 14: As the 4th row.

Row 15: P1, T3F, T3B, P2, T3F, T3B, P1.

Row 16: As the 2nd row.

Row 17: As the 1st row.

Row 18: As the 2nd row.

Row 19: As the 3rd row.

Row 20: As the 4th row.

Row 21: P1, [K2, P2] twice, K2, sl the last 6 sts worked onto the cn and wrap the yarn 4 times counter-clockwise around these 6 sts, then sl these 6 sts back onto the right-hand needle, P2, K2, P1.

Row 22: As the 4th row.

Row 23: As the 15th row.

Row 24: As the 2nd row.

Repeat these 24 rows for pattern.

BACK:

With smaller needles cast on 84 (88, 96, 100, 108) sts. Work in K2, P2 ribbing for 2 inches. Change to larger needles and set up pattern as follows:

Row 1: *P9 (10, 12, 13, 15) sts, pm, work row 1 of twisted and crossed cable pattern over the next 16

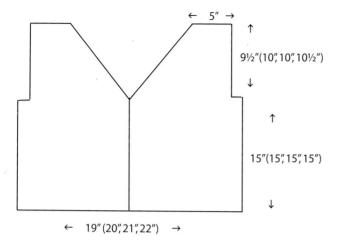

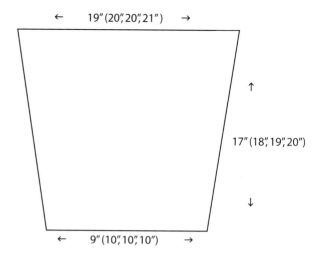

sts, pm, repeat from * twice more, end with P9 (10, 12, 13, 15).

Row 2: *K9 (10, 12, 13, 15) sts, slip marker, work row 2 of twisted and crossed cable over next 16 sts, slip marker, repeat form * twice more, end with P9 (10, 12, 13, 15).

Continue to work in patterns as established until the piece measures 14 (15, 15, 16, 16) inches or desired length to underarm. End with a WS row.

SHAPE ARMHOLES:

Bind off 6 (7, 8, 9, 10) sts at the beg of the next 2 rows. Continue in patterns as established until armhole measures 9 (10, 10, 11, 12) inches. Place all sts on a holder.

LEFT FRONT:

With smaller needles cast on 42 (44, 48, 50, 54) sts. Work in K2, P2 ribbing for 2 inches.

Change to larger needles and set up pattern as follows:

Row 1: P9 (10, 12, 13, 15) sts, pm, work row 1 of twisted and crossed cable over the next 16 sts, pm,

P17 (18, 20, 24, 28) sts.

Row 2: K17 (18, 20, 24, 28) sts, slip marker, work row 2 of twisted and crossed cable pattern over the next 16 sts, slip marker, K9 (10, 12, 13, 15) sts.

Work in patterns as established until piece measures 14 (15, 15, 16, 16) inches or desired length to underarm, ending with a WS row.

SHAPE ARMHOLE AND NECK:

Bind off 6 (7, 8, 9, 10) sts at the beg of the next row.

Decrease row: K1, SSK, work in pattern to end of row. Work 3 rows even. Repeat the decrease row. Repeat these last 4 rows 9 (10, 11, 12, 13) times. 26 (26, 28, 28, 30) sts remain. Work even in pattern if necessary to the same length as the back. Place all sts on a holder.

RIGHT FRONT:

With smaller needles cast on 42 (44, 48, 50, 54) sts and work in K2, P2 ribbing for 2 inches.

Change to larger needles and set up patterns as follows:

Row 1: P17 (18, 20, 24, 28), pm, work row 1 of

twisted and crossed cable pattern over the next 16 sts, pm, P9 (10, 12, 13, 15) sts.

Row 2: K9 (10, 12, 13, 15) sts, slip marker, work row 2 of twisted and crossed cable over the next 16 sts, slip marker, K17 (18, 20, 24, 28) sts.

Continue in patterns as established to the same length to the underarm, ending with a RS row.

SHAPE ARMHOLE AND NECK:

Bind off 6 (7, 8, 9, 10) sts at the beg of the next row, work in pattern to the last 3 sts; K2tog, K1. Work 3 rows even. Work to the last 3 sts of the next row, K2tog, K1. Repeat the last 4 rows 9 (10, 11, 12, 13) times more. Work even if necessary to the same length as the back.

Join the shoulder sts using the three needle bind off method as described in the *Glossary*.

SHAWL COLLAR:

With circular needle and RS facing, starting at the bottom of the right front, pick up and K3 sts for every 4 rows along the neck edge. Place a marker on the needle at the beg of the neck shaping. Pick up 3 sts for every 4 rows along the neck edge, K across the sts from the back neck holder, pick up 3 sts for every 4 rows along left front neck edge, place a marker at the beg of the neck shaping, pick up 3 sts for every 4 rows along the left front edge to the bottom. Work in K2, P2 ribbing across all sts for 2 rows.

BEGIN SHORT ROWS:

Work in ribbing to 2 sts before the second marker, wrap and turn, work in ribbing to 2 sts before the remaining marker, wrap and turn. Work in ribbing to 4 sts before the next marker, wrap and turn, work to 4 sts before the next marker, wrap and turn. Continue to leave 2 more sts before each marker until there are 22 (24, 26, 28, 30) sts being left before each marker. Work across all sts picking up the wraps and knitting them together with the sts when you come to them. This will take 2 rows to do.

BUTTONHOLE ROW:

Mark the right front band with safety pins for 6 buttonholes evenly spaced, having one buttonhole at the start of the neck shaping and one buttonhole 3 sts up from the bottom edge. Continue in ribbing pattern, bind off 2 sts for each buttonhole on the next row. Cast on 2 sts at each buttonhole space on the following row. Work 2 more rows. Bind off all sts. Fold collar and steam lightly to set the fold.

SLEEVES:

With smaller needles cast on 36 (38, 40, 42, 42) sts. Work in K2, P2 ribbing for 3 inches. Change to larger needles and work in reverse St st. Increase 1 st at the beg and end of every 4th row until there are 72 (80, 80, 88, 96) sts. Work even until sleeve measures 16 (17, 18, 18, 19) inches or desired length to underarm. Bind off all sts loosely.

FINISHING:

With right sides together match the center of the sleeve to the shoulder seam, pin the outer edge of the sleeve to the corners of the front and back. Back stitch in place. Sew the bound off sts of the front and back to the upper sleeve seam then continue sewing the sleeve seam. Sew side seams. Sew on buttons to match the buttonholes.

classic guernsey

There have been times when it seemed like everyone in Northampton was knitting this sweater. It is a favorite knitting project of many beginning knitters since it is simple to make and so comfortable to wear. It is based on a very traditional design, but the bulky yarn and simple shaping make it a quick to knit project. The oversized fit means it looks great on both men and women.

SIZES: S (M, L)

FINISHED MEASUREMENTS: 40 (44, 48)"/102 (112, 122) cm

MATERIALS: 8 (9, 10) Lamb's Pride Bulky from Brown Sheep Company (85% wool, 15% mohair; 125 yds/100 gms)

NEEDLES: One pair size 10 (6 mm) and 10½ (6.5 mm), 16" circular needle size 10 (6 mm), yarn needle, 2 stitch holders.

GAUGE: 14 sts and 20 rows = 4" in St st

BACK:
With smaller needles cast on 72 (76, 84) sts. Work in K1, P1 ribbing for 2 inches. Change to larger needles and work in St st until piece measures 6 (7, 8) inches. K 6 rows.

Work in garter st and double moss st as follows: (See *Tip on page 54*)

Row 1: K4, *K2, P2 across to last 4 sts, K4.
Row 2: K4,* P2, K2 across to last 4 sts, K4.
Row 3: K4, *P2, K2 across, to last 4 sts, K4.
Row 4: K4, *K2, P2 across to last 4 sts, K4.

Repeat these 4 rows until piece measures 21 (23, 24) inches. Place all sts on a holder.

FRONT:
Work as for back until piece measures 18 (20, 21) inches.

SHAPE NECK:
Work in pattern as established for 30 (31, 35) sts, place the center 12 (14, 14) sts on a holder. Attach a second ball of yarn and work in pattern as established over the last 30 (31, 35) sts. Working both sides at once and keeping continuity of pattern, decrease 1 st at each neck edge 5 (6, 7) times. 25 (25, 28) sts remain.

Join front to back using the three needle bind off method as described in the *Glossary.*

SLEEVES:
With smaller needles cast on 40 (42, 44) sts. Work in K1, P1 ribbing for 2½ inches. Change to larger needles and work in St st for 4 rows. Increase 1 st at the beginning and end of the next and every following 4th row 14 (16, 17) times, 70 (76, 80) sts. Work even in St st until sleeve measures 17 (18, 19) inches or desired length to underarm. Bind off all sts loosely.

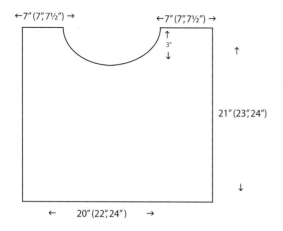

←7" (7", 7½") →   ←7" (7", 7½") →

↑
3"
↓

↑

21" (23", 24")

↓

← 20" (22", 24") →

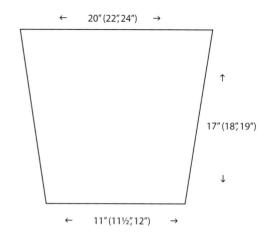

← 20" (22", 24") →

↑

17" (18", 19")

↓

← 11" (11½", 12") →

FINISHING:

Neckband: With circular needle, K across the 22 (26, 28) sts from the back neck holder, pick up and K 10 (12, 14) sts down left front neck edge, K across sts from front neck holder, pick up and K 10 (12, 14) sts up right front neck edge. Work in K1, P1 ribbing for 3 inches. Bind off all sts loosely.

Measure down 10 (11, 12) inches from shoulder seams on both front and back and mark for underarm.

Sew sleeves to front and back, matching center of sleeve to shoulder seam and matching edge of sleeves to underarm markers. Sew side and underarm seams.

❖ **TIP** ❖   When working the double moss stitch it is easy to keep track of the pattern by marking the RS rows with a pin or colored yarn tie. From then on the RS rows are always worked by doing the opposite of what you see. If the stitch is a K then P it, if the stitch is a P then K it. All of the WS rows are worked as they appear. If the stitch is a K then K it, if the stitch is a P then P it. Using this tip means that you will no longer have to keep track of the 4-row pattern, you will be able to "read" your knitting.

bonnie's basketball pullover

Bonnie Otto has been the secretary to the men's basketball team at the University of Massachusetts for a very long time. She has been caught on TV knitting at the basketball games and has been known to have at least four projects at a time on needles. Bonnie is shown wearing the results on the court at UMass in the Mullins Center. If you ever get to a UMass basketball game you may just spot Bonnie knitting in the stands.

SIZE: S (M, L, XL)

FINISHED MEASUREMENTS: 36 (38, 40, 42)"/91.5 (96.5, 102, 107) cm

MATERIALS: 13 (14, 15, 16) sks Rapture by JCA (50% silk, 50% wool; 72 yds/50gms); 2 sks Galaxy by JCA (62% nylon, 38% poly; 51 yds/50 gms)

NEEDLES: Size 8 (5 mm) straight needles, one 16" circular size 8 (5 mm), 2 stitch holders, yarn needle

GAUGE: 16 sts and 28 rows = 4" in stitch pattern

PURL DASH PATTERN:
Row 1: (RS) *K4, P6, repeat from * across.
Rows 2, 4, 6, 8: Purl.
Rows 3 and 7: Knit.
Row 5: P5, *K4, P6 repeat from * across.

BACK:

With size 8 needle and MC, cast on 72 (76, 80, 84) sts. Work in garter st for 12 rows. Change to Purl Dash Pattern, beginning with row 1 and work even until piece measures 10 (11, 11½, 12) inches or desired length to underarm. End with a WS row.

SHAPE ARMHOLES:

Bind off 4 sts at the beginning of the next 2 rows. Decrease 1 st at each end of every other row 4 (5, 6, 7) times. 56 (58, 60, 62) sts remain. Work even, maintaining continuity of pattern until armhole measures 6 (6½, 7, 7½) inches ending with a WS row.

SHAPE NECK:

Work across 15 (16, 17, 18) sts in pattern, attach a second ball of yarn and bind off the center 26 sts. Continue across the remaining sts in pattern. Working both sides at once, bind off 3 sts at each neck edge 3 times. Work even in pattern until armhole measures 8 (8½, 9, 9½) inches. Place all sts on a holder.

FRONT:

Make a second piece exactly as for the back.

Join the shoulder sts using the three needle bind off method as described in the *Glossary.*

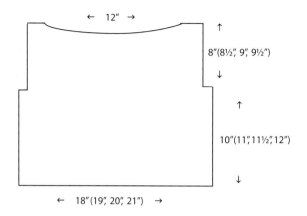

← 12" →

8"(8½", 9", 9½")

10"(11", 11½", 12")

← 18" (19", 20", 21") →

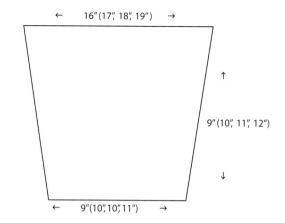

16" (17", 18", 19")

9" (10", 11", 12")

← 9"(10", 10", 11") →

SLEEVES:

With CC and size 8 needles, cast on 40 (42, 44, 46) sts. K1 row, P1 row. Change to MC and work in Purl Dash Pattern for 6 rows. Increase 1 st at beginning and end of the next and every following right side row 12 (13, 14, 15) times, keeping increased sts in Purl Dash Pattern. There are now 64 (68, 72, 76) sts. Work even in pattern as established until sleeve measures 9 (10, 11, 12) inches or desired length to underarm, ending with a WS row.

SHAPE ARMHOLE:

Bind off 4 sts at the beginning of the next 2 rows. Decrease 1 st at each end of every other row 5 (6, 7, 8) times. Bind off all sts loosely.

NECK BAND:

With RS facing and CC pick up and K in each st all around neckline. Place marker for beg of round and K3 rounds. Bind off all sts loosely.

Sew sleeves to body, matching center of sleeve to the shoulder seam and matching bound off sts at underarms.

Sew side and sleeve seams. Work in ends.

4. stitch Pattern Sweaters

ADD SOME TEXTURE TO A SIMPLE SHAPE AND the results can be stunning. The designs in this section all feature stitch patterns that complement the basic construction. Simple seed stitch, a more involved brick stitch, or a repetitive cable can help bring out the best in a yarn. Two of these sweaters are done in a super bulky yarn so the knitting is fast and the results are fun to wear.

brick stitch pullover

Manos del Uruguay has been dyeing wool for many years. When they began to kettle-dye cotton the results were spectacular. The kettle dyeing results in a subtle variation in the color that gives the garment an interesting and unique look. The cotton shows off the stitch pattern and creates a soft and comfortable fabric.

SIZES: S (M, L, XL)

FINISHED MEASUREMENTS: 38 (42.5, 45.5, 50)"/ 96.5 (108, 115.5, 127) cm

MATERIALS: 8 (9, 10, 11) sks Manos Cotton Stria by Design Source (100% cotton; 116 yds/50 gms)

NEEDLES: One pair size 5 (3.75 mm) and one 24" circular needle size 5 (3.75 mm), yarn needle, 2 stitch holders

GAUGE: 20 sts = 4" and 12 rows = 1¾" in pattern on size 5 needles

BRICK PATTERN (multiple of 8+2)
Twelve row repeat.
Row 1 and 7: (RS) Knit.
Row 2 and 8: K1 (edge st), P to last st, K1.
Row 3 and 5: K1 (edge st) * P3, K2, P3, repeat from * to last st, K1.
Row 4 and 6: K1 (edge st) * K3, P2, K3, repeat from * to last st, K1.
Row 9 and 11: K1 (edge st) *K1, P6, K1, repeat from * to last st, K1.

Row 10 and 12: K1 (edge st) * P1, K6, P1, repeat from * to last st, K1.

BACK:
With size 5 needles, cast on 98 (106, 114, 122) sts. Work in brick stitch pattern until piece measures 12 inches, ending with row 6 or 12 of pattern. Bind off 8 sts at beg of next 2 rows. 82 (90, 98, 106) sts. Continue in pattern until armhole measures 8.5, (9, 9.5, 10) inches.

Short row shoulder shaping: *Work across sts in pattern to the last 10 sts, wrap and turn, (sl next st, move yarn between needles, sl st back to the left-hand needle and turn the work). Repeat from the * once. Work to the last 20 sts then wrap and turn; repeat once. Work to the last 30 sts, wrap and turn; repeat once. 30 sts have been left on each shoulder for every size. Place remaining 22 (30, 38, 46) sts on a holder for the back neck.

FRONT:
Work as for the back until armhole measures 2 inches.

Divide for neck: Work in pattern over 40 (44, 48, 52) sts, place the next 2 sts on a safety pin, join a second ball of yarn and work the remaining sts. Working both sides at once, maintaining brick stitch pattern as established, decrease 1 st at each neck edge on next and then every 3rd row 9 (13, 17, 21) times. Work even until piece measures 8.5 (9, 9.5, 10) inches. Work short rows as follows:

Right front piece: Start the short rows on a RS row,

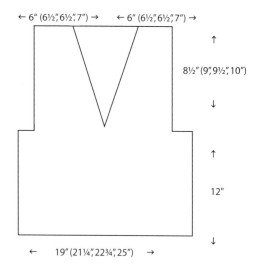

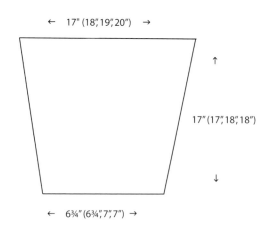

leaving 10 sts at the end of next RS row, then leave 20 sts at the end of the following RS row. Work one more row. Place all sts on a holder.

Left front piece: Start the short rows on a WS row, leaving 10 sts at the end of next WS row. Then leave 20 sts at the end of the following WS row. Work one more row. Place all sts on a holder.

SLEEVES:

Cast on 38 (42, 42, 42) sts. Work in brick stitch pattern for 2½ inches. Increase 1 st at each end of next and then every 4th row 18 (20, 22, 24) times, incorporating the new sts into the brick stitch pattern. Work even in pattern until sleeve measures 17 (17, 18, 18) inches, or desired length to underarm. Bind off all sts loosely.

FINISHING:

Join shoulder seams using the three needle bind off method as described in the *Glossary.*

NECK:

With right side facing and circular needle, knit across the sts from the back neck holder, pick up and K 2 sts for every 3 spaces along left front neck edge, place marker, K2tog from the safety pin, place marker, pick up and K 2 sts for every 3 spaces along right front neck edge. Place a marker for end of rnd.

Rnd 1: P to 2 sts before first center front marker, P2tog, slip marker, P1, remove marker, P2tog, P to end of round.

Rnd 2: K to 2 sts before center front marker, K2tog, slip marker, K1, SSK, K to end.

Rnd 3: Repeat rnd 1.

Rnd 4: Bind off all sts in K, decreasing 1 st as in rnd 2 at center front.

Sew sleeves to body, matching center of top of sleeve to shoulder seam. Sew underarm and side seams. Work in all ends.

autumn jacket

This is an easy to knit jacket done with very little shaping. The lapels are formed by simply folding back the fronts and adding a collar. The color variations in the wool make it an unusual piece while the knitting remains easy and quick on large needles.

FINISHED MEASUREMENTS: 38 (42, 46, 50)"/96.5 (107, 117, 127) cm

MATERIALS: 11 (12, 13, 14) sks Handpaint Wool by Plymouth Yarns (100% wool; 66 yds/100 gms), or 11 (12, 13, 14) sks Yukon (35% wool, 35% mohair, 30% acrylic; 60 yds/100 gms), three 1" buttons

NEEDLES: Size 15 (10mm) needles or size needed to obtain gauge, 3 stitch holders, yarn needle

GAUGE: 10 sts and 12 rows = 4"

SEED STITCH PATTERN:
Row 1: K1, P1 across row.
Row 2: P the K sts and K the P sts.
  Repeat these 2 rows for pattern.

BACK:
With size 15 needles cast on 44 (48, 52, 56) sts and work in seed stitch pattern until piece measures 20 inches. Place all sts on a holder.

LEFT FRONT:
Cast on 22 (24, 26, 28) sts and work in pattern as follows:
Row 1: (RS) K1, P1 across.
Row 2: (WS) Sl 1 wyif, K1, P1 across.
  Mark the RS of the piece with a safety pin.
  Repeat these 2 rows until piece measures 20 inches, end having completed Row 1.
  Next Row: Bind off 9 sts, work to end of row and place remaining 13 (15, 17, 19) sts on a holder.

RIGHT FRONT:
Cast on 22 (24, 26, 28) sts and work in pattern as follows:
Row 1: (RS) Sl 1 wyib, P1, K1 across.
Row 2: (WS) P1, K1 across.
  Mark the RS of the piece with a safety pin.
  Repeat these 2 rows until piece measures 5 inches, end having completed Row 2.
  Buttonhole Row: Sl 1 wyib, P1, yo, P2tog, seed st to end.
  Continue in pattern until piece measures 9 inches. Repeat buttonhole row. Continue in pattern until piece measures 13 inches. Repeat buttonhole row. Continue in pattern until piece measures 20 inches, end having completed Row 2.
  Next Row: Bind off 9 sts, work to the end of row and place remaining 13 (15, 17, 19) sts on a holder.

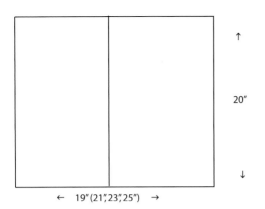

20″

← 19″ (21″, 23″, 25″) →

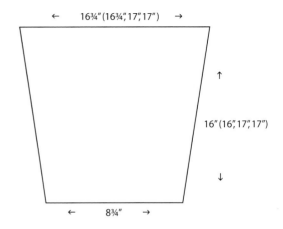

← 16¾″ (16¾″, 17″, 17″) →

16″ (16″, 17″, 17″)

← 8¾″ →

SLEEVES:

Cast on 22 sts and work in seed st until piece measures 2 inches. Increase 1 st at each end of the next row and then every following 6th row until there are 42 (42, 44, 44) sts. Work even until sleeve measures 16 (16, 17, 17) inches or desired length. Bind off all sts.

FINISHING:

With right sides together join fronts to back using the three needle bind off method as described in the *Glossary.*

Collar: With RS facing, beginning at the 4th bound off st of right front neck edge, pick up and K 6 sts from neck edge, 1 stitch in the shoulder seam, K across the 18 sts from the back neck, pick up and K 1 stitch in the shoulder seam and pick up and K 6 sts along bound off edge of left neck. Work in seed st, increase 1 st at each end of every other row 6 times. Bind off all sts loosely.

Sew sleeves to body. Sew side and underarm seams. Sew on buttons to match buttonholes. Work in ends. Fold back bound off sts of fronts at neck to form lapels.

side-to-side pullover

Starting at one cuff and working across to the other cuff is a lesson in both increasing and decreasing. The bottom bands are picked up and ribbed after the front and back have been completed. This is a lot of sweater to have in your lap, but the results are worth it. The two colors add drama to the sweater and the cable up the sleeves and around the neck accentuate the long line of cuff-to-cuff knitting.

SIZES: One size fits most

FINISHED MEASUREMENTS: 44"/112 cm

MATERIALS: Giotto by Colinette (50% cotton, 40% rayon, 10% nylon; 155 yds/100 gms), 1 sk in color A, 4 sks in color B

NEEDLES: One size 10½ (6.5 mm) 24" circular needle, 1 cable needle, yarn needle

GAUGE: 12 sts and 16 rows = 4"

CABLE PATTERN (worked over 6 sts)
Row 1, 3, 7, 9: K2, P2, K2.
Row 2, 4, 6, 8, 10: P2, K2, P2.
Row 5: Slip 4 sts onto cable needle and hold in back, K2, slip the 2 P sts from the cable needle back to the left-hand needle and P them, then K2 sts from the cable needle.
Repeat these 10 rows for pattern.

STARTING WITH THE SLEEVE CUFF:
With color A cast on 32 sts. Work in K1, P1 ribbing for 2 inches.

SET UP CABLE PATTERN:
Next row: (RS) P13 sts, place marker, work row 1 of cable pattern over the next 6 sts, place marker, P13 sts.
Row 2: (WS) K13, sl marker, work row 2 of cable pattern over next 6 sts, sl marker, K13.
Row 3: P13, cable row 3, P13.
Row 4: K13, cable row 4, K13.

Continue in cable pattern, keeping all other sts in reverse St st. Increase 1 st at the beg and end of every 4th row 17 times, working the increased sts in reverse St st.

SHAPE BODY:
Cast on 30 sts at the beginning of the next 2 rows. Work in reverse St st and cable pattern for another 8 rows. Change to color B and work in patterns as established for next 30 rows.

DIVIDE FOR NECK: Work across 54 sts, bind off the center 18 sts, work remaining sts. (54 sts on each side.)

BACK: Work even on last 54 sts for 24 rows. Place sts on a holder and return to the first 54 sts. Attach yarn and working on these sts, decrease 1 st at the neck edge every other row 3 times. Work even for 12 rows. Cast on 1 st at the neck edge every other row 3 times. Knit 1 row.

JOIN FRONT AND BACK: Work across front, ending at the neck edge. Cast on 18 sts onto the right-hand needle, then P across the sts from the back.

REESTABLISH CABLE PATTERN:

K60 sts, pm, work cable pattern row 2 over next 6 sts, pm, K to end.

Next Row: P to marker, work cable pattern row 3 over next 6 sts, sl marker and P to end.

Next Row: K to marker, work cable pattern row 4 over next 6 sts, sl marker, K to end.

Continue in patterns as established until a total of 30 rows from the front and back joining have been completed.

Keeping continuity of pattern, bind off 30 sts at the beg of the next 2 rows. Decrease 1 st at the beg and end of every 4th row 17 times. Work 4 rows even in pattern. Work 2 inches of K1, P1 ribbing. Bind off in ribbing.

BOTTOM RIBBINGS:

With right side of back facing, pick up and K 82 sts along bottom edge. Work 12 rows in K1, P1 ribbing. Bind off in ribbing. Repeat along the bottom edge of front.

Sew side and sleeve seams, pinning to match carefully.

NECKBAND:

Cast on 11 sts.

Row 1: P2, work row 1 of cable pattern over next 6 sts, P3.

Row 2: K3, work row 2 of cable pattern over next 6 sts, K2.

Row 3: P2, work row 3 of cable pattern over next 6 sts, P3.

Row 4: K3, work row 4 of cable pattern over next 6 st, K2.

Continue in patterns as established until 110 rows have been completed. Bind off all sts. Sew bound off edge to cast on edge. With right sides facing, pin neck band to neck edge easing in the fullness of the neck to fit the band, placing the neck band seam at the center back. Sew band to neck with a back stitch.

celtic plait pullover

One day a customer came into the shop and asked to have a sweater made that she could give as a gift. It needed to be fairly simple, but still have some cables in it to reflect the Irish heritage of the person she would be giving it to, her priest. When it was finished, she was pleased and the priest was very happily surprised. Since then this sweater has been made for many different individuals, but I often think of that priest wearing this sweater in acknowledgment of his parishioner's thanks.

SIZES: S (M, L, XL)

FINISHED MEASUREMENTS: 38 (42, 46, 50)"/96.5 (107, 117, 127) cm

MATERIALS: 11 (12, 13, 14) sks Frog Tree Worsted Weight Alpaca from T&C Imports, (100% alpaca; 87 yds/50 gms)

NEEDLES: Size 5 (3.75 mm) and 7 (4.5 mm) straight needles, one 16" circular needle size 5 (3.75 mm), cable needle, 2 stitch holders, yarn needle

GAUGE: 20 sts and 24 rows = 4" in double seed st on size 7 needles

DOUBLE SEED STITCH:
Row 1: K1, P1 across desired number of sts.
Row 2: K the Ks and P the Ps as they appear.
Row 3: P1, K1 across desired number of sts.
Row 4: P the Ps and K the Ks as they appear.
  Repeat these 4 rows for pattern.

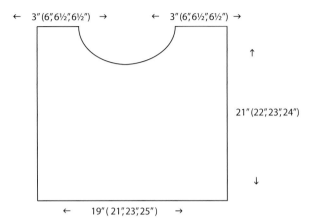

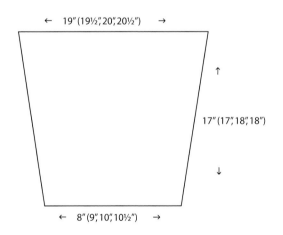

CELTIC CABLE PATTERN (worked over 33 sts)
First foundation row: (RS) P4, K3, *P4, K6, repeat from * to last 6 sts, P6.

colinette baby jacket

Every baby deserves a little color, and this little jacket is the perfect way to provide it. The smallest size uses just one skein of Colinette Point Five, which is available in a rainbow of colors. The jacket has become a favorite because it is quick to knit; many of my customers have done it in a weekend. Give it as a shower gift and it will be sure to impress everyone.

An easy pattern.

SIZES: 6 months (1 year, 2 years)

FINISHED MEASUREMENTS: 18½ (25½, 28½)"/47 (65, 72.5) cm

LENGTH TO SHOULDER: 9½ (11, 14)"/24 (28, 35.5) cm

SLEEVE LENGTH: 7 (9, 12)"/18 (23, 30.5) cm

GAUGE: 10 sts = 4" in St st on size 15 needles

MATERIALS: 1 (2, 2) sks hand-dyed Colinette Point Five (100% hand-dyed wool; 54 yds/100 gms), 1 (2, 2) sks Brown Sheep Lamb's Pride Bulky (85% wool, 15% mohair; 125 yds/100 gms)

NEEDLES: Size 10½ (6.5 mm) and 15 (10 mm) knitting needles, yarn needle, 4 buttons, 3 stitch holders

BACK:
With size 10½ knitting needles and Lamb's Pride Bulky, cast on 28 (32, 36) sts. Work in K1, P1 ribbing for 5 rows. On next row of ribbing decrease 5 sts evenly spaced across row. 23 (27, 31) sts remain. Change to size 15 knitting needles and Point Five and work in St st until piece measures 9½ (11, 14) inches. Place all sts on a holder.

LEFT FRONT:
With size 10½ knitting needles and Lamb's Pride Bulky, cast on 13 (15, 17) sts. Work 5 rows in K1, P1 ribbing. On next row of ribbing, dec 1 (1, 1) st. 12 (14, 16) sts remain. Change to size 15 knitting needles and Point Five and work in St st until piece measures 7 (8½, 11½) inches, ending with a RS row.

NECK SHAPING:
On next row, bind off 3 sts, then dec 1 st at neck edge every row until 6 (8, 10) sts remain. Work even if necessary until piece measures 9½ (11, 14) inches. Place rem sts on holder.

RIGHT FRONT:
Make a piece as for left front, but begin neck shaping on a K row.

SLEEVES: (make 2)
With size 10½ knitting needles and Lamb's Pride Bulky, cast on 18 (22, 26) sts. Work 6 rows in K1, P1 ribbing. Change to St st and increase 1 st at each end of every 4th row 5 (7, 8) times. 26 (34, 40) sts rem. Work even until piece measures 7 (9, 12) inches. Bind off all sts loosely.

Second foundation row: K6, *P6, K4, repeat from * to the last 7 sts, P3, K4.

Row 1: P4, K3, *P4, C6F (slip next 3 sts to cable needle and hold in front, K3, then K3 from the cable needle) repeat from * to the last 6 sts, P6.

Row 2: K6, * P6, K4, repeat from * to the last 7 sts, P3, K4.

Row 3: P4, *T5F (slip the next 3 sts to the cable needle and hold in front, P2, then K3 sts from the cable needle), T5B (slip the next 2 sts to the cable needle and hold in back, K3, then P2 from the cable needle), repeat from * to the last 9 sts, T5F, P4.

Row 4: K4, P3, *K4, P6, repeat from * to the last 6 sts, K6.

Row 5: P6, *C6B (slip the next 3 sts to the cable needle, hold in back, K3, then K3 from the cable needle), P4, repeat from * to the last 7 sts, K3, P4.

Row 6: As the 4th row.

Row 7: P4, *T5B, T5F, repeat from * to the last 9 sts, T5B, P4.

Row 8: As the 2nd row.

Repeat these last 8 rows for pattern.

BACK:

With smaller needles, cast on 95 (105, 115, 125) sts. Work in K1, P1 ribbing for 2 inches. Change to larger needles and work in double seed st until piece measures 21 (22, 23, 24) inches. Place all sts on a holder.

FRONT:

With smaller needles, cast on 95 (105, 115, 125) sts and work in K1, P1 ribbing for 2 inches. Increase 32 (30, 32, 30) sts evenly spaced across the last row of ribbing, 127 (135, 147, 155) sts.

SET UP PATTERNS:

Work 7 (9, 11, 14) sts in row 1 of double seed st pattern, place marker, work 33 sts in first foundation row of Celtic cable pattern, place marker, 7 (9, 11, 14) sts in row 1 of double seed st pattern, place marker, work 33 sts in first foundation row of Celtic cable pattern, place marker, 7 (9, 11, 14) sts in row 1 of double seed st pattern, place marker, 33 sts in first foundation row of Celtic cable pattern, place marker 7 (9, 11, 14) sts in row 1 of double seed st pattern.

Next Row: *Work row 2 of double seed st pattern to marker, work 2nd foundation row of Celtic cable to the next marker, repeat from * across row, ending with the last 7 (9, 11, 14) sts in row 2 of the double seed st.

Next Row: *Work row 3 of double seed st pattern to marker, work row 1 of Celtic cable pattern to the next marker, repeat from * across row, ending with the last 7 (9, 11, 14) sts in row 3 of double seed st pattern.

Next Row: *Work row 4 of double seed st pattern to marker, work row 2 of Celtic cable pattern to the next marker, repeat from * across ending with the last 7 (9, 11, 14) sts in double seed stitch pattern.

Note: What makes this pattern so very knitter-friendly is that all of the WS rows are worked as the sts appear. If it looks like a K, knit it, if it looks like a P, purl it, in both pattern sts.

Continue in patterns as established, repeating rows 1 through 8 of the Celtic cable pattern and rows 1 through 4 of the double seed st pattern until the piece measures 18 (19, 20, 21) inches.

SHAPE NECK:

Work across 47 (51, 57, 61) sts in pattern, place the center 33 sts on a holder, attach a second ball of yarn and work across remaining 47 (51, 57, 61) sts in patterns as established.

Working both sides at the same time, decrease 1 st at each neck edge of every other row 8 times. 39 (43, 49, 53) sts remain, end with a WS row.

Next row: Decrease 9 sts evenly spaced across this last row by knitting 2 tog. 30 (34, 40, 44) sts remain for each shoulder.

Join shoulder sts using the three needle bind off method as described in the *Glossary.*

SLEEVES:

With smaller needles, cast on 43 (47, 51, 53) sts. Work in K1, P1 ribbing until piece measures 3 inches. Increase 10 (12, 14, 16) sts evenly spaced across last row of ribbing. 53 (59, 65, 69) sts.

SET UP ROW:

Work 10 (13, 16, 18) sts in double seed st, place marker, work 33 sts in first foundation row of Celtic cable pattern, place marker, work remaining 10 (13, 16, 18) sts in double seed st pattern.

Next row: Work 10 (13, 16, 18) sts in row 2 of double seed st pattern, work 33 sts in 2nd foundation row of Celtic cable pattern, work last 10 (13, 16, 18) sts in row 2 of double seed st pattern.

Continue in patterns as established, working rows 1–8 of Celtic cable pattern over the center 33 sts. Increase 1 st at each end of every 4th row 18 (20, 22, 24) times, working the increased sts into the double seed st pattern. There are 89 (99, 109, 117) sts. Work even in patterns as established until sleeve measures 17 (17, 18, 18) inches. Bind off all sts loosely.

Measure from the shoulder seam down the front and the back 9 (10, 11, 11½) inches and place a pin. Sew sleeves to body, matching the center of the sleeve to the shoulder seam and the underarms of the sleeve to the pins on the body. Sew the side and underarm seams.

NECK FINISHING:

With RS facing, using the circular needle and starting at the back, K across the 35 (37, 35, 37) sts from the back neck holder, pick up and K 10 (12, 14, 16) sts down left front neck edge, K across the 33 sts from the front neck holder, and pick up and K 10 (12, 14, 16) sts up the right front neck edge. Place a marker for the beginning of the round and work in K1, P1 ribbing for 2 inches. Bind off all sts loosely. Weave in ends.

double cable pullover

My husband is a sweater lover. He often wears a sweater instead of a coat. He watches me knit for other people and wonders out loud who the next sweater is for, all the time looking hopefully at the basket of yarn at my feet. I designed and knit this sweater for him to wear on special occasions. He loves the softness and warmth of the alpaca. The cables add just enough to keep the knitting interesting without adding a lot of bulk to the garment.

SIZES: S (M, L, XL, XXL)

FINISHED MEASUREMENTS: 42 (44, 46, 48, 50)"/106.5 (112, 117, 122, 127) cm.

MATERIALS: 15 (16, 17, 18, 19) sks Frog Tree Chunky Alpaca by T and C Imports (100% alpaca; 54 yds/50 gms)

NEEDLES: One pair size 9 (5.5 mm) and size 10 (6 mm), one 16" circular needle size 9 (5.5 mm), yarn needle, stitch holders, cable needle

GAUGE: 14 sts and 16 rows = 4" in St st on size 10 needles

CABLE PANEL:
Row 1: P2, K6, P2, K10, P2, K6, P2.
Row 2 and all even rows: K2, P6, K2, P10, K6, P2.
Row 3: P2, C6B (slip 3 sts to cn and hold in back, K3, K3 from the cable needle), P2, K10, P2, C6B, P2.
Row 5: P2, K6, P2, C10B (slip 5 sts to cn and hold in back, K5, K5 from the cn), P2, K6, P2.

Row 7: As row 1.
Row 9: As row 3.
Row 11: As row 5.
Row 12: As row 2.
   Repeat these 12 rows for pattern.

BACK:
With smaller needles cast on 74 (78, 80, 84, 88) sts. Work in K2, P2 ribbing for 3 inches. Change to larger needles and work in St st until piece measures 16 (17, 18, 19, 20) inches or desired length to underarm. End with a WS row.

SHAPE ARMHOLES:
Bind off 4 sts at the beg of the next 2 rows.
   Decrease Row: K2, SSK, K to the last 4 sts, K2tog, K2.
   Purl the next row. Repeat these 2 rows 5 (6, 7, 8, 9) times. Work even until armhole measures 9 (10, 10, 11, 12) inches. Place all sts on holder.

FRONT:
With smaller needles cast on 80 (84, 86, 90, 104) sts. Work in K2, P2 ribbing for 3 inches. Change to larger needles and set up pattern as follows:
Row 1: K 25 (27, 28, 30, 37) sts, pm, work row 1 of cable pattern over the next 30 sts, pm, K25 (27, 28, 30, 37) sts.
Row 2: P25 (27, 28, 30, 37) sts, slip marker, work row 2 of cable pattern over the next 30 sts, slip marker, P25 (27, 28, 30, 37) sts.

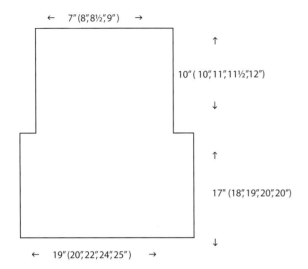

← 7"(8", 8½", 9") →

10"(10", 11", 11½", 12")

17" (18", 19", 20", 20")

← 19"(20", 22", 24", 25") →

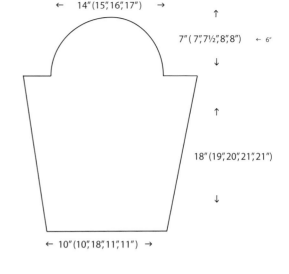

← 14"(15", 16", 17") →

7"(7", 7½", 8", 8")   ← 6"

18"(19", 20", 21", 21")

← 10"(10", 18", 11", 11") →

Continue in patterns as established until piece measures the same as the back to the underarm. Shape armholes the same as for the back. Work even until armhole measures 7 (8, 8, 9, 10) inches.

SHAPE NECK:

Work 23 (24, 24, 25, 31) sts in pattern, slip the next 14 sts to a holder. Attach a second ball of yarn and work across the remaining 23 (24, 24, 25, 31) sts.

Working both sides at once, decrease 1 st at each neck edge on every other row 5 times. Work even on remaining 18 (19, 19, 20, 26) sts until piece measures same length as back to the shoulder. Join the front and back using the three needle bind off.

SLEEVES:

With smaller needles cast on 34 (34, 36, 36, 38) sts and work in K2, P2 ribbing for 3 inches. Increase 6 sts

evenly spaced across the last row of ribbing. Change to larger needles and set up pattern as follows:

Row 1: K5, pm, work cable pattern over the next 30 sts, pm, K5.

Row 2: P5, slip marker, work row 2 of the cable pattern over the next 30 sts, slip marker, P5. Continue in pattern as set, increasing 1 st at the beg and end of the next and then every following 4th row 14 (15, 16, 17, 18) times. Work new sts in St st. Work even until sleeve measures 17 (17, 18, 19, 20) inches or desired length to underarm. Bind off 4 sts at the beg of the next 2 rows.

Decrease row: K2, SSK, work in pattern to the last 4 sts, K2tog, K2.

Work one row. Repeat these last 2 rows until sleeve cap measures 6 (7, 8, 9) inches. Bind off all sts.

NECK:

With circular needle, knit across the sts from the back neck, pick up and K 8 (10, 10, 12, 14) sts down left front neck, P2, K10, P2 across the sts from the front holder, pick up and K 8 (10, 10, 12, 14) sts up the right front neck edge. Place a marker for the beg of the round and work in K2, P2 ribbing and continuing the cable pattern over the sts on the front neck until the ribbing measures 3 inches. Bind off all sts loosely.

FINISHING:

Match center of sleeves to the shoulder seam. Match bound off sts at each underarm and sew in place. Sew side and underarm seams. Work in ends.

adult dot cardigan

This is an adult-sized version of the dot cardigan pattern for children. The softly spun, super bulky yarn makes this a great jacket for those blustery New England days. The stitch pattern is simple to knit but fools the eye. Everyone thinks this is a more complicated pattern than it is, and marvels at the way the purl stitches seem to form squares in the knitting.

SIZE: S (M, L, XL, XXL)

FINISHED MEASUREMENTS: 38 (40, 44, 48, 52)"/96.5 (102, 112, 122, 132) cm

MATERIALS: 5 (5, 6, 7, 8) sks of Magnum by Cascade Yarns (100% wool; 123 yds/100 gms)
6¾-inch buttons

NEEDLES: One pair size 15 (10 mm) needles, stitch holders, yarn needle

GAUGE: 9 sts and 12 rows = 4"

PATTERN STITCH:
Row 1: *K3, P1, repeat from * across.
Row 2: Purl.
Row 3: K1, *P1, K3, repeat from * across.
Row 4: Purl.

BACK:
With size 15 needles cast on 42 (44, 46, 48, 50) sts. Work in garter stitch (K every row) for 5 rows. Change to dot pattern as follows:
Row 1: *K3, P1, repeat from * across ending with K2 (4, 2, 4, 2).
Row 2: Purl.

Row 3: K1, *P1, K3, repeat from * across ending with K4 (2, 4, 2, 4).
Row 4: Purl.

Work even in pattern as established until piece measures 10 (11, 12, 13, 14) inches or desired length to underarm. End with a WS row.

SHAPE ARMHOLE:
Bind off 4 sts at the beginning of the next 2 rows.

Work even in pattern as established until armhole measures 9 (9, 10, 10, 11) inches, ending with a WS row.

Next row: Bind off the center 16 (16, 18, 18, 20) sts. Purl 1 row on each shoulder. Place remaining sts on a holder.

LEFT FRONT:
Cast on 21 (22, 23, 24, 25) sts. Work in garter st for 5 rows. Change to dot pattern as follows:
Row 1: *K3, P1, repeat from * ending with K1 (2, 3, 0, 1).
Row 2: Purl.
Row 3: K1, *P1, K3, repeat from * ending with K3 (4, 1, 2, 3).
Row 4: Purl.

Work even to same length as back to underarm ending with a WS row.

SHAPE ARMHOLE:
Bind off 4 sts at the beginning of the next row. Work even in pattern as established until armhole measures 6 (6, 7, 7, 8) inches, ending with a RS row.

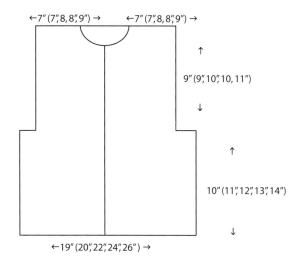

←7" (7", 8", 8", 9") →   ←7" (7", 8", 8", 9") →

9" (9", 10", 10, 11")

10" (11", 12", 13", 14")

←19" (20", 22", 24", 26") →

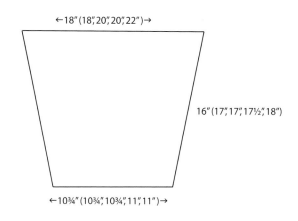

←18" (18", 20", 20", 22")→

16" (17", 17", 17½", 18")

←10¾" (10¾", 10¾", 11", 11")→

SHAPE NECK:

Bind off 5 (5, 6, 6, 7) sts at the beginning of the next row. Work 1 row. Decrease 1 st at the beginning of the next and every other row 3 (3, 4, 4, 5) times. 9 (10, 10, 11, 11) sts remain. End with a WS row and place sts on a holder.

RIGHT FRONT:

Work as for left front but end with a RS row at the underarm. End with a WS row to start the neck shaping.

SLEEVES:

Cast on 24 (24, 24, 26, 26) sts. Work in garter stitch for 7 rows. Change to pattern stitch and work 4 rows. Increase 1 st at each end of the next and every following 4th row until there are 42 (42, 44, 44, 46) sts. Work even until sleeve measures 16 (17, 17, 17½, 18) inches, or desired length to underarm. Bind off all sts.

FINISHING:

Join shoulders using the three needle bind off method as described in the *Glossary*.

With RS of left front facing, pick up and K3 sts for every 4 rows along front edge. K 5 rows. Bind off. With RS of right front facing, pick up and K 3 sts for every 4 rows along front edge. K 2 rows. Make 5 buttonholes evenly spaced on the next row by doing a yo, K2tog. K 2 more rows and bind off. With RS facing, pick up and K 3 sts for every 4 rows around the neck. K 2 rows. K to the last 4 sts of the next row, yo, K2tog, K2. K 2 more rows. Bind off. Sew on buttons to match buttonholes.

Match the center of the sleeve to the shoulder seam, match ends of sleeve to the corner of the bind off at the underarm. Sew sleeve to body. Sew each side of the sleeve to the bound off sts of the front and back. Sew underarm and side seams. Weave in ends.

5. the Birth of a Baby Store

"YOU NEED A BIGGER STORE."

"You really have yarn in every inch of this space!"

"You could sure use more room."

If I heard a comment like this once, I heard it many, many times. In 2002 Northampton Wools was feeling like a closet. Every inch of space was being utilized to store yarn, and model sweaters were hanging from every section of the ceiling.

In September 2003 the doors of Northampton Wools, Too were opened right next door to Northampton Wools. This is a second space devoted entirely to babies and children.

From the very first day Northampton Wools, Too has met with enthusiasm and excitement. Expectant mothers enter the shop eager to make that special sweater for the coming baby; grandmothers come in looking for yarn to knit a blanket. Locals and visitors to the town shop for that unique hand-knit item to give as a gift, knowing each item has been crafted with care.

All the extra space has meant that I have been able to create and design items exclusively for babies and children. I have included the most popular of these designs in this chapter. These patterns have been tested by many knitters over the years and have proven themselves to be favorites of both the knitters and the wearers. Most of them are simple enough for even the beginner knitter and will knit up quickly.

Opening Northampton Wools, Too really has been like giving birth. I hope this sampling of patterns brings you joy and happiness.

blossom stripe

A colorful play of stripes accents the bottom of the body and the sleeves of this easy-to-knit pullover. The boat neck shaping allows the sweater to pop on quickly over every head. It is shown in colorways appropriate for either a girl or a boy and I would encourage the knitter to experiment with the colors. New mothers will appreciate the washability of the yarn, while the babies will cuddle up in its softness.

An easy pattern.

SIZES: 3–6 months (9–12 months, 18–24 months, 3 years, 4 years)

FINISHED CHEST SIZES: 21 (23, 25, 27, 29)"/53.5 (58.5, 63.5, 68.5, 73.5) cm

LENGTH TO SHOULDER: 9 (10, 11, 13, 14)"/23 (25.5, 28, 33, 35.5) cm

SLEEVE LENGTH: 6 (8, 10, 11, 12)"/15 (20.5, 25.5, 28, 30.5) cm

MATERIALS: Reynolds Blossom (50% acrylic, 40% viscose, 10% cotton; 82 yds/50 gms), 1 sk each of color A, B, and C, and 2 (2, 3, 4, 4) sks of color D

NEEDLES: Size 6 (4 mm) and 8 (5 mm) needles, or size necessary to obtain gauge; crochet hook size G, stitch holder, tapestry needle

GAUGE: 18 sts and 20 rows = 4" in St st on size 8 needles

BACK:
With smaller needles and color C cast on 50 (54, 68, 62, 66) sts and work 4 rows in garter stitch. Change to larger needles, work in St st, and starting with color A, work in striped pattern as follows:
4 rows with color A.
2 rows with color B.
2 rows with color C.
2 rows with color B.

Repeat stripe pattern once more, then work 4 more rows with color A. Change to color D and work even until piece measures 9 (10, 11, 13, 14) inches. Bind off the center 26 (30, 34, 38, 42) sts. Leave remaining sts for each shoulder on a stitch holder.

FRONT:
Work exactly the same as for the back.

Join the shoulders together using the three needle bind off method as described in the *Glossary.*

SLEEVES:
With smaller needles and color C cast on 22 (26, 32, 36, 36) sts. Work 4 rows in garter st, then change to larger needles and St st. Work stripe pattern as given for back, increasing 1 st at each end of every 10th row. Change to color D and continue to increase 1 st at each end every 4th row until there are 32 (36, 42, 46, 50) sts. Work even until sleeve measures 6 (8, 10, 11, 12) inches. Bind off loosely.

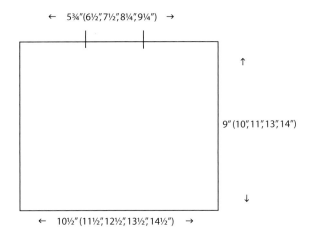

← 5¾"(6½",7½",8¼",9¼") →

9" (10",11",13",14")

← 10½" (11½",12½",13½",14½") →

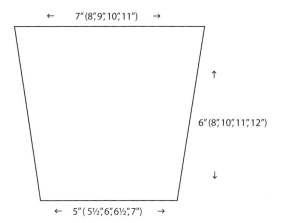

← 7" (8",9",10",11") →

6" (8",10",11",12")

← 5" (5½",6",6½",7") →

FINISHING:

With the right sides together, match the center of the sleeve to the shoulder seam. Pin the top of the sleeve to the edge of the body, making sure to have the same amount of sleeve on each side. Sew in place. Sew the side and underarm seams. With a crochet hook and color C, work a row of single crochet around the neck edge, being careful not to be too tight. Work in ends.

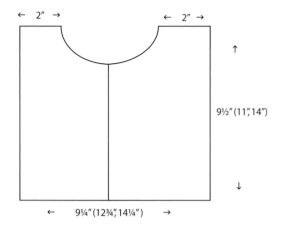

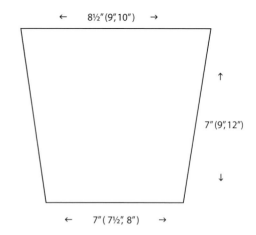

FINISHING:

Join the shoulders using the three needle bind off method as described in the *Glossary*.

BUTTON BAND: With size 10½ knitting needles and Lamb's Pride Bulky, pick up and K 26 (29, 32) sts along left front edge. Work in K1, P1 ribbing for 5 rows. Bind off all sts loosely.

BUTTONHOLE BAND: With size 10½ knitting needles and Lamb's Pride Bulky, pick up and K 26 (29, 32) sts along right front edge. Work 2 rows in K1, P1 ribbing. On next row, work in buttonholes as follows:

BUTTONHOLE ROW: Rib 6 (7, 8) sts, yo, K2tog, [rib 6 (7, 8) sts, yo, K2tog] twice, rib 2 sts.

Work 2 more rows in K1, P1 ribbing. Bind off all sts loosely.

NECK BAND: With size 10½ knitting needles and Lamb's Pride Bulky, pick up and K 37 (43, 47) sts around neck edge. Work 2 rows in K1, P1 ribbing.

Next Row: Rib across row to last 4 sts, yo, K2tog, rib 2.

Work 2 rows in K1, P1 ribbing. Bind off all sts loosely.

Sew sleeves to body, then sew sides of body and underarms. Sew buttons onto button band opposite buttonholes.

cotton striped cardigan and pullover

My sister's twins love to wear the sweaters I make for them as long as Valerie's is pink and Justin's is blue. Styled as either a cardigan or a pullover, the stripes can be subtle as in the blue, or contrasted as in the pink. The rolled edges make a comfortable fit at the cuffs and add a touch of fashion to this easy-to-knit duo.

An easy pattern.

SIZES: 1 (2, 3, 4) years

FINISHED MEASUREMENTS: 22 (24, 26, 28)"/56 (61, 66, 71) cm

LENGTH TO SHOULDER: 11 (12, 13, 14)"/28 (30.5, 33, 36) cm

SLEEVE LENGTH: 8 (9, 10, 11)"/20 (23, 25.5, 28) cm

MATERIALS: Plymouth Fantasy Natural (100% cotton, 140 yds/100gms) 2 (2, 3, 3) sks each of color A and color B

NEEDLES: *Both sweaters:* Size 6 (4 mm) and 8 (5 mm), and 11 (7 mm) needles, one 16" circular needle size 6 (4 mm)
Cardigan: 3 stitch holders, yarn needle, 5 buttons

GAUGE: 16 sts = 4" in St st on size 8 needles

> ❖ **TIP** ❖ When working in stripes that require frequent changes of color, do not cut the yarns. Just carry each color up the side of the piece.

Cardigan and Pullover

BACK:
With smaller needle and color A, cast on 44 (48, 52, 56). Starting with a knit row, work 4 rows in St st. Work 6 rows in K2, P2 ribbing. Change to larger needles and work in stripe pattern as follows:

4 rows in St st with color A.

2 rows in St st with color B.

Work even in stripe sequence until piece measures 11 (12, 13, 14) inches. Place all sts on a holder.

PULLOVER FRONT:
Work as for back until the piece measures 8 (9, 10, 11) inches, ending with a WS row.

SHAPE NECK: K across 17 (18, 19, 20) sts. Sl the next 10 (12, 14, 16) sts to a stitch holder. Attach a second ball of yarn and knit across the remaining 17 (18, 19, 20) sts. Keeping the continuity of the stripe pattern and working both sides at the same time, decrease 1 st at each neck edge on every knit row 4 (5, 6, 7) times. Work even if necessary on the remaining 13 sts until the front measures 11 (12, 13, 14) inches.

Join the front shoulder sts to the back shoulder sts using the three needle bind off.

SLEEVES:
With smaller needles and color A cast on 28 (30, 32, 34) sts. Starting with a K row, work 4 rows in St st. Work 6 rows in K2, P2 ribbing. Change to larger needle and work in stripe sequence as given for back,

increasing 1 st at each end of every 4th row 9 (10, 11, 12) times. 46 (50, 54, 58) sts. Continue in stripe pattern, work even until sleeve measures 8 (9, 10, 11) inches. Bind off all sts loosely.

FINISHING FOR PULLOVER:
Sew sleeves to body, matching center of sleeve to shoulder seam. Sew side and underarm seams.

NECKBAND: With RS facing, use circular needle and color B to K across the 18 (22, 26, 30) sts from the back neck holder, pick up and K8 (9, 12, 13) sts down the left front, K across the 10 (12, 14, 16) sts from front neck holder, and pick up and K8 (9, 12, 13) sts up the right front. 44 (52, 64, 72) sts total. Place marker and work 4 rounds in K2, P2 ribbing. Work 4 rounds in St st (K every round). Bind off all sts loosely.

❖ **TIP** ❖ To insure that the sts are bound off loosely enough to fit easily over a child's head, use a needle at least three sizes larger than what was used for knitting.

Cardigan

LEFT FRONT:
With smaller needle and color A cast on 22 (24, 26, 28) sts. Starting with a K row work 4 rows in St st. Work 6 rows in K2, P2 ribbing. Change to larger needles and continue in stripe pattern as given for back. Work even until piece measures 6 (7, 8, 9) inches, ending with a K row.

SHAPE NECK: Decrease 1 st on the next and every following 4th row 9 (11, 13, 15) times. 13 sts remain for every size. Work even if necessary until front measures 11 (12, 13, 14) inches. Place sts on a holder.

RIGHT FRONT:
Work as for left front, but end with a P row before the neck shaping.

Join shoulder sts using the three needle bind off method as described in the *Glossary.*

FRONT BAND: With RS facing and beginning at the bottom of the right front, use circular needleand color B to pick up and K 3 sts for every 4 rows up the right front neck edge, K across the sts from the back neck holder and pick up and K 3 sts for every 4 rows down the left front. Work 2 rows in K2, P2 ribbing. On the next row make 5 buttonholes by working a yo, K2tog at evenly spaced intervals on the right front for a girl and the left front for a boy. Work 2 more rows of ribbing. Change to St st and work 4 rows. Bind off all sts loosely. Sew on buttons to match buttonholes.

FINISHING:
Sew in sleeves. Sew underarm and side seams. Weave in ends.

child's dot cardigan and hat

The body of this cardigan is done in one piece so there are no side seams to sew. The stitch pattern is simple to do but looks more complicated than it is. It is a quick knit on large needles and can be made for a girl or a boy. Knitting the hat makes this popular outfit complete.

An intermediate pattern.

SIZES: 2 (4, 6, 8, 10)

FINISHED MEASUREMENTS: 22 (24, 26, 28, 30)"/56 (61, 66, 71, 76.5) cm

LENGTH TO SHOULDER: 11½ (13, 14½, 16, 18)"/29 (33, 37, 41, 46) cm

SLEEVE LENGTH: 8 (9, 10, 11, 12)"/20 (23, 25.5, 28, 30.5) cm

MATERIALS: 3 (4, 4, 5, 6) sks Plymouth Yarns Encore Mega (75% acrylic, 25% wool; 64yds/100 gms) 4 buttons

NEEDLES: Size 11 (8 mm) and 13 (9 mm) needles, 3 stitch holders, yarn needle

GAUGE: 10 sts and 13 rows = 4"

PATTERN STITCH:
Row 1: (RS) *P1, K3, repeat from * across.
Row 2: Purl.
Row 3: K2, *P1, K3, repeat from * across.
Row 4: Purl.
   Repeat these 4 rows for pattern.

BODY:
With smaller needles cast on 48 (52, 56, 60, 64) sts. P1 row, K1 row, P1 row. Change to larger needles and work in pattern st starting with row 1, until piece measures 6 (7, 8, 9, 10) inches or desired length to underarm, ending with a WS row.

DIVIDE FOR BACK AND FRONTS:
Keeping continuity of pattern, work 12 (13, 14, 15, 16) sts for right front. Place remaining sts on a holder. Work even in pattern st as established on sts for right front until armhole measures 4 (4½, 5, 6, 7) inches, ending with a WS row.

SHAPE NECK:
Bind off 4 (4, 5, 6, 7) sts at beginning of next row. Continue in pattern, decrease 1 st at the neck edge every other row 2 (2, 2, 3, 3) times. Work even if necessary until armhole measures 5½ (6, 6½, 7, 8) inches. Place all sts on a holder for shoulder.

BACK:
With right side facing, rejoin yarn and keeping continuity of pattern, work across the next 24 (26, 28, 30, 32) sts from holder. Continue in pattern stitch as established until armhole measures 5½ (6, 6½, 7, 8) inches. Place all sts on a holder.

LEFT FRONT:
With RS facing rejoin yarn to remaining 12 (13, 14, 15, 16) sts on holder and work as for right front. Work neck shaping at the beginning of a WS row.
   Join shoulders using the knitted seam method.

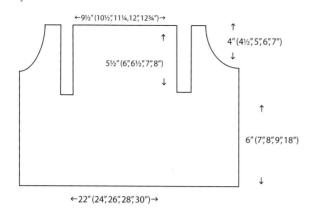

←9½"(10½",11¼",12",12¾")→

4"(4½",5",6",7")

5½"(6",6½",7",8")

6"(7",8",9",18")

←22"(24",26",28",30")→

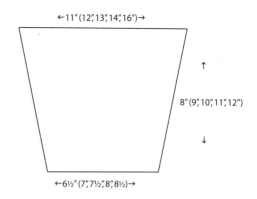

←11"(12",13",14",16")→

8"(9",10",11",12")

←6½"(7",7½",8",8½")→

SLEEVES:

With smaller needles cast on 16 (18, 20, 22, 24) sts. P1 row, K1 row, P1 row. Change to larger needles and continue in pattern st starting with row 1. Increase 1 st at each end of every 4th row, working increased sts into pattern, until there are 28 (30, 32, 34, 36) sts. Work even until sleeve measures 8 (9, 10, 11, 12) inches.

Bind off all sts loosely.

FINISHING:

With size 11 needles and RS of left front facing, pick up and K 30 (34, 38, 42, 46) sts along the front edge. K 3 rows. Bind off. With RS of right front facing, pick up and K the same number of sts along front edge. K 1 row.

Next row: Make 4 buttonholes as follows: K2 * yo, K2tog, K5 (6, 7, 8, 9) sts, repeat from * to end of row. K 1 row. Bind off. With RS facing and beginning at right front, pick up and K26, (28, 30, 32, 34) sts around neck edge. K 1 row.

Next row: K2, yo, K2tog, K to end. K 1 more row then bind off.

Sew sleeve seams. Set sleeves into body, matching center of sleeve to shoulder seam and sleeve seam to underarm of body.

Sew on buttons to match button holes.

Hat

SIZE: S (6–12 months), M (2–3 years), L (4 years and up)

MATERIALS: Encore Mega, 1 sk in color A and 1 sk in color B

NEEDLES: Size 13 (9 mm) straight needles

GAUGE: 10 sts = 4"

With size 13 needles and color A cast on 40 (44, 48) sts. Knit 7 rows.

Change to color B and begin pattern as follows:
Row 1: Purl.
Row 2: *K3, P1, repeat from * across row.
Row 3: Purl.
Row 4: K1, *P1, K3, repeat from * across.

Repeat these 4 rows for pattern until piece measures 6 (7, 8) inches, ending with Row 1 or 3.

K2tog across next row. P2tog across next row. Cut yarn leaving a 15-inch tail. Thread yarn through all remaining sts and pull tightly. Sew the back seam of the hat. Work in ends.

duck pullover

The Eric Carle Museum of Picture Book Art is located just across the river from Northampton. We were able to use the museum as a backdrop when photographing the projects in the children's section of this book thanks to our friend Chrissy Noh, the marketing manager at the museum. Just as we were getting ready to photograph the sweaters, Eric Carle's Ten Little Rubber Ducks *was released. I imagine we were both under the same stars when inspiration hit.*

SIZES: 6 months (12 months, 18 months, 24 months)

FINISHED MEASUREMENTS: 20 (22, 24, 26)"/51 (56, 61, 66) cm

LENGTH TO SHOULDER: 11 (12, 13½, 14½)"/28 (30.5, 34, 37) cm

SLEEVE LENGTH: 7 (7½, 8, 8½)"/18 (19, 20.5, 21.5) cm

GAUGE: 22 sts & 28 rows = 4"

MATERIALS: Tahki Yarns Cotton Classic (100% cotton; 109 yds/50 gms), 4 (4, 5, 5) sks of main color, 1 sk of yellow, 1 sk of blue. Black embroidery floss to embroider the eye

NEEDLES: Size 5 (3.75 mm) and 6 (4 mm) or size needed to obtain gauge, 16" circular needle size 5 (3.75 mm), 3 stitch holders, tapestry needle

BACK:

With smaller needles and main color cast on 56 (60, 66, 70) sts. Work in K1, P1 ribbing until piece measures 1 inch. Change to larger needles and work in St st until piece measures 11 (12, 13½, 14½) inches. Place all sts on a holder.

FRONT:

With smaller needles and main color, cast on 56 (60, 66, 70) sts. Work in K1, P1 ribbing until piece measures 1 inch. Change to larger needles, work 4 rows in St st with blue.

Work the 52 sts from the chart on page 96, reading the chart from right to left on the K rows and left to right on the P rows. For rows 1–5 work the remaining 4 (8, 14, 18) sts in blue, then for the remaining rows of the chart work them in the MC. When chart is complete continue in MC until piece measures 9½ (10, 10½, 11) inches, ending with a WS row.

SHAPE NECK:

Knit across 20 (21, 23, 24) sts, place next 16 (18, 20, 22) sts onto a holder, attach a second ball of yarn and knit the remaining 20 (21, 23, 24) sts. Working both sides at once, decrease 1 st at the neck edge on every knit row 5 (6, 7, 8) times. Leave sts on the needle.

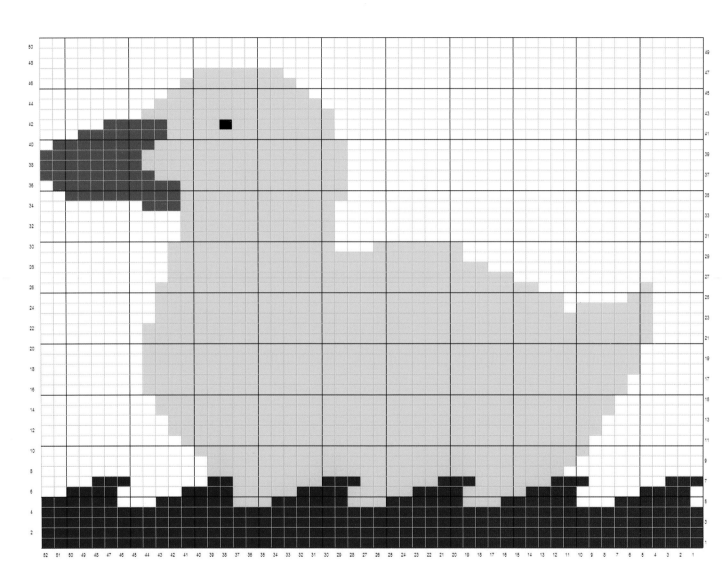

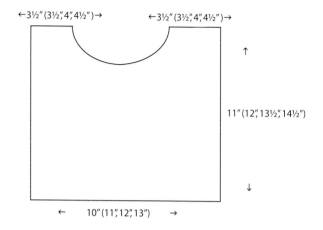

←3½" (3½", 4", 4½")→   ←3½" (3½", 4", 4½")→

11" (12", 13½", 14½")

←   10" (11", 12", 13")   →

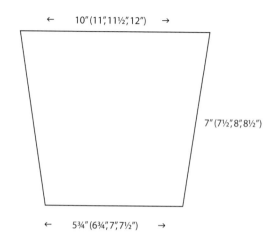

←   10" (11", 11½", 12")   →

7" (7½", 8", 8½")

←   5¾" (6¾", 7", 7½")   →

JOIN SHOULDERS:

Place 15 (15, 16, 16) from the back holder onto a needle. Hold the front and back together with right sides together and bind off the shoulder sts using the three needle bind off method as described in the *Glossary*. Repeat for the second set of shoulder sts, leaving the 26 (30, 34, 28) sts on the holder for the back neck.

SLEEVES:

With smaller needles and main color cast on 32 (38, 40, 42) sts. Work in K1, P1 ribbing for 1½ inches. Change to larger needles and continue in St st, increasing 1 st at each end of the next row, then on every 4th row until there are 56 (60, 64, 68) sts. Work even until sleeve measures 7 (7½, 8, 8½) inches. Bind off all sts loosely.

FINISHING:

Pin center of sleeve top to the shoulder seam, right sides together. Measure down 5 inches (5½, 5¾, 6) on the front and back from the shoulder seam, then pin sleeve to fit those measurements. Sew sleeve to body. Sew side and underarm seams. Work in all ends, closing any holes that may have occurred in the color work.

NECK:

With right side facing, using the 16" circular needle, knit the sts from the back neck holder. Pick up and K10 (12, 14, 16) sts along the left side of neck, K across the sts from the front neck holder, pick up and K10 (12, 14 16) sts along the right-hand side of the neck. Place a marker on needle. Work in rounds of K1, P1 for 1½ inches. Bind off all sts loosely.

fandango fun baby cardigan

*When I met Susan Shabo I knew she was special
and I count myself blessed to have her as a friend.
Susan is a designer and yarn sales representative in
New England so I see her often. She has always
found ways to encourage the creation of new ideas
and is quick to hand out patterns for the yarns with
which we all love to knit. A note or card from Susan
means there will be a little pattern for a scarf or hat
included. Her patterns and ideas have been
favorites of customers for a long time and her
encouragement and support have meant much to
me. She very generously offered this baby cardigan
pattern, which has been very popular in the mother-
to-be set. The cardigan uses only one skein of
Fandango from Colinette Yarns and knits up very
quickly. It is soft and cuddly and every baby will be
very happy to own one.*

SIZE: 6 months–1 year

MATERIALS: Colinette Fandango (100% cotton; 108
yds/100 gms), 3 buttons

NEEDLES: Size 9 (5.5 mm) and 10½ (6.5 mm)
needles

GAUGE: 8 sts = 4" (Make sure to match this gauge. If
the knitting is too tight there will not be enough
yarn).

BACK:
With smaller needles, cast on 21 sts loosely. Work in
St st for 1 inch. Change to larger needles and continue
in St st until piece measures 9 inches. Bind off 6 sts at
the beg of the next two rows. Place remaining sts on a
holder.

FRONTS:
With smaller needles, cast on 9 sts loosely. Work in St
st for 1 inch. Change to larger needles and continue in
St st until piece measures 6½ inches.

SHAPE NECK FOR LEFT FRONT:
Bind off 2 sts at the beginning of the next P row. Knit
one row. Decrease 1 st at the beginning of the next
row. Work even until piece measures the same as the
back. Bind off all sts.

SHAPE NECK FOR RIGHT FRONT:
Bind off 2 sts at the beginning of the next knit row.
Purl one row. Decrease 1 st at the beginning of the
next row. Work even until piece measures same as the
back. Bind off all sts.

Sew shoulder seams. Measure down 4½ inches
from the shoulder seam on front and back and mark
with pins.

SLEEVES:
With larger needles and RS facing, pick up and K 19
sts between the pins. Work in St st (beg with a P row)
for 2½ inches. Decrease 1 st at beg and end of needle
on the next row, then every 4th row 2 more times. 13
sts remain. When sleeve measures 6 inches in length,
change to smaller needles and continue for 1 inch.
Bind off very loosely.

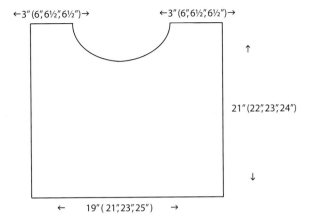

←3″(6″,6½″,6½″)→ ←3″(6″,6½″,6½″)→

21″(22″,23″,24″)

← 19″(21″,23″,25″) →

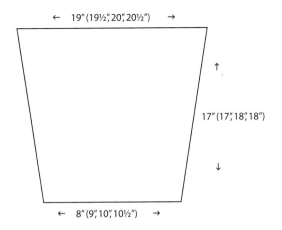

← 19″(19½″,20″,20½″) →

17″(17″,18″,18″)

← 8″(9″,10″,10½″) →

LEFT FRONT BAND: (button band) With RS facing and smaller needles, pick up and K 13 sts along left front edge. Work in St st beg with a P row for 1¼ inches. Bind off loosely.

RIGHT FRONT BAND: (buttonhole band) With RS facing and smaller needles, pick up and knit 13 sts along right front edge. Work in St st, beg with a P row for 1 row.

Next row: K2, *yo, K2tog, K2,* repeat between the *s, end with K1. Continue in St st until band measures 1¼ inches. Bind off loosely.

COLLAR:

With smaller needles and RS facing, starting at the middle of top edge of right front band, pick up and K 9 sts along right front neck edge, knit across 9 sts from the back neck holder, pick up and K 9 sts along left front neck edge, ending at the middle of the left front band (27 sts). Work in St st beg with a knit row for 3 rows. Change to larger needles and continue in St st until collar measures 3 inches. Bind off very loosely.

Sew side and sleeve seams. Sew on buttons.

❖ **TIP** ❖ When ever you need to bind off loosely, just use a larger needle. Don't be afraid to use a needle at least 2 or 3 sizes larger than what you are working with, especially if you tend to bind off tightly to begin with. This is the number one problem knitters have with baby sweaters, so loosen up!

lettuce-edge hat

DESIGNED BY BONNIE OTTO AND LINDA DANIELS

Bonnie and I created this hat to match the Lettuce-Edge Sweater. The large number of stitches that are needed to make the edging can be a challenge to cast on. Use markers every 50 stitches or so to make it easier to count.

SIZES: 6 months (1 year, 2 years, 3–7 years)
For newborns, work pattern for the smallest size (6 months) on size 6 knitting needles, or size 5 for preemies

MATERIALS: 100 (150, 150, 150, 150) yards of DK light worsted weight yarn for MC, 20–30 yds for CC

NEEDLES: 16" circular needle size 7, size 7 double-pointed needles, stitch markers, yarn needle

GAUGE: 5 sts = 1" in St st

With CC cast on 288 (320, 352, 384) sts on circular needle and join, being careful not to twist sts, place stitch marker.

Round 1: Knit.
Round 2: *K1, K1, pull the first knitted stitch over the 2nd knitted stitch and off the needle as in binding off; rep from * to end.
Round 3: Knit.
Round 4: K2tog all around. 72 (80, 88, 96) sts.

Change to MC and work in St st (K every round) until piece measures 4¾ (5, 5½, 6) inches from end of lettuce edging.

Begin decreasing for crown of hat changing to double-pointed needles when necessary:
Round 1: *K6, K2tog; rep from * around.
Round 2: *K5, K2tog; rep from * around.
Round 3: *K4, K2tog; rep from * around.

Repeat this decrease progression (K3, K2tog; K2, K2tog; and so on) until 9 (10, 11, 12) sts remain.

Cut a long tail and thread this tail through the remaining sts and pull up tightly. Weave in all ends.

lettuce-edge cardigan

Ruffles make a statement in this cardigan. Done in contrasting colors, the ruffles add a touch of femininity to an otherwise simple knit. Although the ruffle requires a large number of stitches to be cast on, they are quickly decreased. Make it in cotton for easy washing and wearing, or in an acrylic blend. Use your imagination when it comes to color choices, but what little girl doesn't love pink?

An easy pattern.

SIZES: 3 months (6 months, 12 months, 2T, 3T, 4T)

FINISHED MEASUREMENTS: 18 (20, 22, 24, 26, 28)"/46 (51, 56, 61, 66, 71) cm

MATERIALS: Tahki Yarns Cotton Classic (100% cotton, 109 yds/50 gms). MC: 300 (400, 500, 600, 700, 800) yds; CC: 100–200 yds

NEEDLES: Size 7 (4.5 mm) 24" or 29" circular needle or size needed to obtain gauge; size 7 (4.5 mm) straight needles, size 7 double-pointed needles, stitch holders, yarn needle, stitch markers, 5–7 buttons

GAUGE: 22 sts and 24 rows = 4" in St st on size 7 needles

BACK:

Using the circular needle, with CC cast on 200 (220, 240, 264, 288, 308) sts.

Work in Lettuce Edge pattern as follows:

Row 1: Knit.

Row 2: P2tog across the next row.

Row 3: (sl 1, K1, PSSO) across RS row; 50 (55, 60, 66, 72, 77) sts rem on needle. Change to straight needles.

Work 3 rows in St st starting with a P row (K the RS, P the WS).

Change to MC; continue even in St st until piece measures 10 (11, 12¼, 13, 14, 15) inches from the color change. Place all sts on a holder.

LEFT FRONT:

With CC, cast on 88 (96, 108, 120, 132, 140) sts. Work in Lettuce Edge pattern as for the back; 22 (24, 27, 30, 33, 35) sts rem. Work 3 rows in St st beginning with a P row.

Change to MC and work even in St st until piece measures 8 (9, 10¼, 11, 12, 12½) from the color change **, ending with K (RS) row.

SHAPE NECK:

Cast off 5 (5, 6, 6, 7, 7) sts at beg of next row; 17 (19, 21, 24, 26, 28) sts rem.

Continue in St st, decreasing 1 st at beg of every WS row 4 times.

Work even on rem 13 (15, 17, 20, 22, 24) sts, if necessary, until left front measures the same as the back. Place all sts on a holder.

RIGHT FRONT:

Work as for left front to **, ending with a Purl (WS) row. Shape neck as for left front, but work all bind offs and decreases on the RS (K) row.

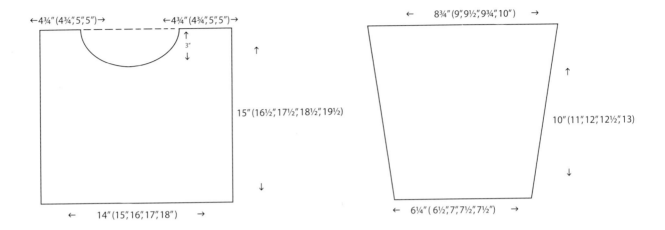

← 4¾" (4¾", 5", 5")→ ← 4¾" (4¾", 5", 5")→ ↑ 3" ↓ ↑ 15" (16½", 17½", 18½", 19½") ↓ ← 14" (15", 16", 17", 18") →

← 8¾" (9", 9½", 9¾", 10") → ↑ 10" (11", 12", 12½", 13) ↓ ← 6¼" (6½", 7", 7½", 7½") →

Join shoulder: Using the three needle bind off method as described in the *Glossary,* join the front shoulder sts to the back shoulder sts.

SLEEVES: (make 2)
With CC, cast on 112 (112, 120, 120, 128) sts.

Work Lettuce Edge pattern as for the back; 28 (28, 30, 30, 32) sts rem. Work 3 rows in St st beg with a P row.

Change to MC and continue in St st, increasing 1 st at each end of every 4th row until there are 48 (50, 52, 54, 60, 66) sts.

Work even in St st until sleeve measures 5 (6, 7, 7½, 7½, 8) inches from MC edge.

Bind off all sts loosely.

NECK RUFFLE:
With the right side facing you and CC, pick up and K 1 st in *every* stitch around the neck edge, beginning at the right front, knitting the sts from the back neck st holder. Purl 1 row.

Next row: Work increase row by knitting into the front and back of every stitch.

Purl next row.
Repeat the increase row.
Purl 1 more row.
Bind off all sts loosely.

LEFT FRONT BAND: With MC and right side of left front facing, pick up and K 3 sts for every 4 rows. *Do not pick up sts along ruffle.* Work in garter st (K every row) for 6 rows. Bind off loosely. Mark this side for 5–7 buttons evenly spaced along 3rd row of garter st.

RIGHT FRONT BUTTONHOLE BAND: With MC and right side of right front facing, pick up and K the same number of sts as on the left front. *Do not pick up sts along ruffle.* K 2 rows of garter st. On the 3rd row, and by working a yo, K2tog for each, create 5–7 buttonholes to match the button markings from the left front band. Work 3 more rows in garter st. Bind off loosely.

FINISHING:

With right sides facing, fold sleeves in half to find exact middle. Match right sleeve center to right shoulder seam and pin half the sleeve down the front and half down the back, being careful to measure the distances so that the front and back of both sides/sleeves are equidistant. Sew sleeves to body. Rep for left sleeve. Sew side and underarm seams. Sew on buttons; work in ends, and steam lightly to block.

abbreviations

* repeat directions following * as many times as indicated

[ ] repeat directions inside brackets as many times as indicated

approx	approximately
beg	begin(ning)
CC	contrast color
cm	centimeter(s)
cn	cable needle
dec	decreasing
K	knit
K2tog	knit 2 stitches together
M1	make one stitch
MC	main color
mm	millimeter(s)
P	purl
P2tog	purl 2 stitches together
pm	place marker
PSSO	pass slip st over
rem	remain(s)(ing)
rep	repeat
rnd(s)	round(s)
RS	right side(s)
sk(s)	skein(s)
sl	slip
SSK	slip, slip knit
st(s)	stitches
St st	stockinette stitch
tbl	through back of loop
tog	together
WS	wrong side (s)
wyif	with yarn in front
wyib	with yarn in back
yd(s)	yard(s)
yo	yarn over

glossary

Bind off: Knit or purl 2 sts, pull the first st over the second st, * knit or purl the next stitch and pull the first stitch over the second. Repeat from * until desired number of stitches have been bound off.

Bind off in ribbing: Work in ribbing as you bind off. (Knit the knit stitches, purl the purl stitches.)

Cable cast on: Insert right-hand needle in first stitch, pull up a loop and place on left needle (1 stitch cast on). Repeat for desired number of stitches.

Cast on: Place stitches on the needle to begin the work. Use either the long tail method or the knitted on method (see your favorite knitting reference book for instructions).

Circular knitting: Knit all rounds.

Decrease: Eliminate 1 stitch in a row.

Garter Stitch: Knit every row. For circular knitting, knit one round, then purl one round.

Increase: Add stitches in a row.

Knitwise: Insert the needle into the stitch as if you were going to knit it.

Make one: With the right needle tip, lift the strand between the last stitch knit and the next stitch on the left-hand needle and place it on the left-hand needle, then knit into back of it. One knit stitch has been added.

Place markers: Place or attach a loop of contrast yarn or purchased stitch marker as indicated.

Pick up and knit (purl): Knit (or Purl) into the loops along the edge.

Purlwise: Insert the needle into the stitch as if you were going to purl.

Reverse stockinette stitch: Purl right-side rows, knit wrong-side rows.

Selvage stitch: Edge stitch that helps make seaming easier.

Slip, Slip, Knit: Slip next two stitches knitwise, one at a time to right-hand needle. Insert tip of left-hand needle into fronts of these stitches, from left to right. Knit them together. One stitch has been decreased.

Slip stitch: An unworked stitch made by passing a stitch from the left-hand to the right-hand needle as if to purl.

Stockinette stitch: Knit right-side rows, purl wrong-side rows. Circular knitting: knit all rounds.

Three needle bind off: With the right side of the two pieces together and the needles going in the same direction, insert a third needle into the first stitch on the front needle and the first st on the back needle and knit them together.* Knit the next two stitches together the same way. Slip the first stitch on the third needle over the second stitch and off the needle. Repeat from * for three needle bind off.

Work even: Continue in pattern without increasing or decreasing.

Yarn over: Make a new stitch by wrapping the yarn over the right-hand needle.

bibliography

Harmony Guide, ed. *Knitting Stitches*. London, England: Lyric Books Limited, 1983.

Marsh, Elizabeth Le Baron. "Jenny Lind in Northampton." *New England Magazine,* May 1892.

Square, Vicki. *The Knitter's Companion.* Loveland, Co.: Interweave Press, 1996.

Vogue Knitting: The Ultimate Knitting Book. New York: Sixth & Spring Books, 2002.

Zacek Bassett, Lynne. "The Needlework of Grace Coolidge." *Piecework Magazine,* July/August 1999.

resources

The following yarn companies generously provided the yarn for the projects in this book. I am very grateful to all of them for their support.

CLASSIC ELITE YARNS
122 Western Ave.
Lowell, MA 01852
www.classiceliteyarns.com

BROWN SHEEP CO
100662 County Rd., #16
Mitchell, NE 69357
www.brownsheep.com

MOUNTAIN COLORS
P.O. Box 156
Corvallis, MT 50828

DESIGN SOURCE
P.O. Box 770
Medford, MA 02155

CASCADE YARNS
1224 Andover Park East
Tukwila, WA 98188
www.cascadeyarns.com

JCA INC/REYNOLDS
35 Scales Land
Townsend, MA 01469-1094
www.jcacrafts.com

KARABELLA
1201 Broadway
New York, NY 10001
www.karabellayarns.com

TAHKI STACEY CHARLES
70-30 80th St #36
Ridgewood, NY 11385
www.tahkistacycharles.com

UNIQUE KOLOURS
28 N. Beacon Hill Rd
Malvern, PA 19355
www.uniquekolours.com

T&C IMPORTS
P.O. Box 1119
East Dennis, MA 12641

PLYMOUTH YARNS
P.O. Box 28
Bristol, PA 19007
www.plymouthyarn.com

WESTMINSTER FIBERS/
ROWAN YARNS
4 Townsend West Unit #8
Nashua, NH 03063

Contact us:
NORTHAMPTON WOOLS
3 & 11 Pleasant St.
Northampton, MA 01060
413-586-4331
1-800-584-0087
www.northamptonwools.com